Developing and Maintaining a Design–Tech Portfolio

D0217779

Developing and Maintaining a Design–Tech Portfolio

A Guide for Theatre, Film, and TV

Rafael Jaen

AMSTERDAM • BOSTON • HEIDELBERG
LONDON • NEW YORK • OXFORD • PARIS
SAN DIEGO • SAN FRANCISCO • SINGAPORE
SYDNEY • TOKYO

Focal Press is an imprint of Elsevier

Property of Library
Cape Fear Comm College
Wilmington, N. C.

Acquisitions Editor: Cara Anderson
Project Manager: Brandy Lilly
Marketing Manager: Christine Degon Veroulis
Cover Design: Mark Bernard
Interior Design: Mark Bernard

Focal Press is an imprint of Elsevier
30 Corporate Drive, Suite 400, Burlington, MA 01803, USA
Linacre House, Jordan Hill, Oxford OX2 8DP, UK

Copyright © 2006, Elsevier Inc. All rights reserved.

No part of this publication may be reproduced, stored in a retrieval system, or transmitted in any form or by any means, electronic, mechanical, photocopying, recording, or otherwise, without the prior written permission of the publisher.

Permissions may be sought directly from Elsevier's Science & Technology Rights Department in Oxford, UK: phone: (+44) 1865 843830, fax: (+44) 1865 853333, e-mail: permissions@elsevier.com. You may also complete your request online via the Elsevier homepage (http://elsevier.com), by selecting "Support & Contact" then "Copyright and Permission" and then "Obtaining Permissions."

∞ Recognizing the importance of preserving what has been written, Elsevier prints its books on acid-free paper whenever possible.

Library of Congress Cataloging-in-Publication Data
Jaen, Rafael.
   Developing and maintaining a design-tech portfolio : a guide for theatre, film, and TV / by Rafael Jaen.
     p. cm.
   Includes bibliographical references and index.
   ISBN-13: 978-0-240-80712-6 (pbk. : alk. paper)
   ISBN-10: 0-240-80712-X (pbk. : alk. paper)   1. Theaters–Stage-setting and scenery.
2. Motion pictures–Setting and scenery.   3. Television–Stage-setting and scenery.
4. Art portfolios–Design.   I. Title.
   PN2091.S8J33 2006
   792'.025—dc22

                                                   2006002693

British Library Cataloguing-in-Publication Data
A catalogue record for this book is available from the British Library.

ISBN 13: 978-0-240-80712-6
ISBN 10: 0-240-80712-X

For information on all Focal Press publications
visit our website at www.books.elsevier.com

06 07 08 09 10 10 9 8 7 6 5 4 3 2 1

Printed in China

**Working together to grow
libraries in developing countries**

www.elsevier.com | www.bookaid.org | www.sabre.org

ELSEVIER   BOOK AID
International   Sabre Foundation

Dedication

To Stephen Brady, for his optimism and vision.
To my students, who create the magic of the theatre.
To my many colleagues, for their teachings, friendship, and inspiration.

Contents

Preface

My passion for portfolio development began a long time ago. First I used an art and architecture portfolio to transfer from a renowned architectural school in South America to the Theatre Design Program at New York University—no small accomplishment for someone who didn't speak English! Second, I used the portfolio to get jobs as a designer, design assistant, and as a technician while I was in college. Every project offered a new opportunity to feature my skills in my showcase. Later, I used my portfolio to expand my career, get new jobs, get accepted into graduate school, and get a teaching position in higher education. Every goal I have set for career development has been dependent on my portfolio.

WHY A COMPREHENSIVE GUIDE?

As I developed and maintained my portfolio, I began to help others with theirs. Teaching has provided me with the best venue for sharing my knowledge and staying current with trends. This helping and teaching process made me aware of the fact that no books on the market are specifically dedicated to the subject of portfolios and how their requirements may vary, depending on what the portfolio is used for. I recognized the need for such a comprehensive guide, and the main objective of this book is to bring excitement to the process of building a portfolio by helping readers plan and develop details, such as personal presentation, page layouts, content variety, aesthetic sequencing, marketing, and next steps. This book contains practical suggestions to aid in the process of creating, developing, and presenting winning design or technology portfolios in the fields of theatre, film, and television. The text provides guidelines covering a wide range of aspects, from the beginner's portfolio to an advanced portfolio, in addition to featuring samples and lists of "do's" and "don'ts" provided by expert professionals in various design and technology fields. The book also gives the reader information about professional organizations that can be useful for networking, organizations that offer portfolio-based scholarships, companies that hire design and technology freelancers, and more. Another objective was to assist the reader in the process of developing a showcase that can be used by the beginner or established professional to apply for graduate school, to pursue new jobs in the field, and for career marketing promotional purposes. To this end, the book is designed as a reference guide, a workbook, and an inspirational tool.

THE PARTS

Part I is dedicated to the realization of effective portfolio showcases, and it identifies the materials and techniques necessary to produce them. The chapters in Part I identify specific requirements by discipline, including scenery, costumes, lighting, and sound, and cover the various portfolio requirements for applying for graduate school admittance, jobs in the field, and professional organization memberships, as well as for promotional purposes. Part II is dedicated to the development and use of digital portfolios and looks at software used in this area. Part III is about presentation and marketing, and it describes how to develop personal presentation techniques, résumés, business cards, and web pages. Part IV offers helpful information about maintaining and updating portfolios. The chapters include real samples from the professional field and "do's" and "don'ts" with comments from experts in each design or technology discipline. Finally, Part V contains biographies of many who have contributed to this book.

This book also includes detailed information on:
- Choosing a portfolio case and learning how to handle it professionally
- Planning project layouts and organization for successful presentations
- Choosing the best page size and type for specific projects
- Choosing the best acid-free sketch layout materials from among those available on the market today
- Labeling, using keys, and storing reference materials
- Developing and maintaining the portfolio
- Using theatrical design or technology digital portfolio programs
- Developing versatile or purpose-specific résumés and business cards
- Presenting oneself in the best light possible (e.g., grooming, appearance, voice articulation, listening, projecting self-confidence, rapport building)

IN CONCLUSION

A theatrical design–tech portfolio is a showcase of a designer or technician's process, resourcefulness, and artistry. This showcase is key in opening new doors and getting into recognized colleges, obtaining scholarships, and getting new jobs in the field. Putting a portfolio together for presentation can seem like an impossible undertaking and it can be a time-consuming and challenging process, but I hope you keep finding this process useful, inspiring, and helpful!

Introduction

At the time that I finished graduate design school as a costume designer, a portfolio was a fairly uncomplicated affair. It consisted of a case: leather if you could afford it, plastic or fabric covered if you could not. We had all been encouraged to draw large sketches in school, so our portfolios were, out of necessity, also large, usually measuring 24″ × 36″. Inside they were equipped with flimsy plastic pages, which we eventually replaced with the infinitely preferable, but also significantly heavier polypropylene (vinyl) pages.

The rules set-up were simple: produced work in the front, class projects in the back, strongest work first, update it regularly, and be prepared to show it *anywhere*.

Although the guide lines for assembling and maintaining a portfolio were straight-forward, my classmates and I spent countless hours working and re-working our sketches, poring over and selecting photographs, reorganizing layouts, and critiquing each other's work. Before long, opportunities arose to present our portfolios to obtain work as costume designers and assistants.

I showed my portfolio *everywhere*. I showed it to producers in their offices, to designers in their studios and costume shops and to directors wherever I could. I showed it sitting on the floors of rehearsal rooms. I even showed it in restaurants. "Oh! Do you do weddings?" the waitress exclaimed looking at my production of *Faust*. I found that directors always asked about the other directors, and producers always asked about budgets. Costume designers always looked the most carefully and asked the widest range of questions.

Every time I showed my portfolio I came across something to remove and thought of something new to include, so I managed to keep it regularly updated. The advent of color copying, and resizing capabilities added to the flexibility I needed to refurbish my portfolio. Suddenly, I could show many more sketches in much less space. I could include work from more shows, even my research. The possibilities were endless.

I had been out of school for many years when I found that the need to show my portfolio to get work was lessening. Because I was looking at it less frequently, I was not maintaining it as regularly. And, gradually, I found I had less and less time to devote to its upkeep although the amount of material I wanted to include was increasing.

As a guest lecturer, however, I was frequently asked to display my portfolio to students. Although somewhat outdated, it was the perfect layout, with the perfect amount of content to display in the space of an hour, the average amount of time for such a presentation.

Although in a display setting, I seemed to achieve the ideal length and layout, there still remained a considerable amount of material that I had yet to add and my portfolio was already extremely heavy (I practically needed the services of a sherpa to help me carry it around); It seemed impossible to include everything, and I discovered an even greater dilemma in the question of what exactly I wanted to show. I found I no longer knew how I wanted to represent myself through my portfolio.

For many years I had been reviewing portfolios for the USA 829 costume exam. Initially, the exam consisted not only of this review, but also more importantly, an extensive home project which was legendary for it's ability to terrorize applicants. At that time, the portfolio was only half the equation.

A few years ago the home project for costume designers in the eastern region of the United States was eliminated. It was determined that the costume business had changed. Designers no longer had to demonstrate that they could design a wide range of events chosen by the exam committee. If they were being hired for jobs with companies that had a collective bargaining agreement with IATSE USA 829, had both a portfolio that fulfilled the union requirements, and three letters of recommendation, they were qualified to join. The exam committee laid out the new portfolio requirements very carefully. In their eyes at least, the portfolio gained a new level of importance.

The portfolio requirements are specific; applicants are not encouraged to put too much energy into making a concise book for presentation to our panel of reviewers. Instead we ask to see two complete projects for which the applicant has been the principal costume designer or first assistant within the past two years. These projects must include a full set of swatched, full-color sketches, production photos, bibles and research. We also want to see other projects, spread out around a table or stacked up in groups, as well as supporting production photos, research and bibles if the project has been produced.

Even as I was helping students and young designers prepare their portfolios for work and union interviews, as well as graduate school applications, my own portfolio quandary loomed large. I wondered about the possibilities. Maybe I should consider a smaller portfolio? Did I need an archival portfolio? What about digital? A friend sent me a copy of a portfolio she was sending out for revue for a tenure position. It had pages and pages of scanned sketches, photos and design statements. It was beautiful. On the other hand, another friend had dispensed with portfolios altogether, and just took a large sheaf of sketches with him to his interviews.

What does one do, I wondered, when one is changing direction and there are no longer teachers and classmates to turn to for feedback? How does one think objectively about one's portfolio?

When I heard about Rafael's book I was delighted. My own dilemma aside, I am aware that not all schools can devote an entire year or even a semester to portfolio concerns. Discussions of portfolio creation and presentation often occur at the end of a student's academic career when they are busy trying to finish their final projects. When they finally have time to work on their portfolio, their teachers may not be available for comment and critique.

Rafael's book is exhaustive in its treatment of the whole topic of portfolio composition. He very carefully covers all the various types of portfolios and the strengths and weaknesses of each. He presents different types of layout, details the materials necessary to create each one, and lists sources for those materials. He examines the differences between traditional hard portfolios and digital portfolios. He covers resume writing, business cards and promotional materials, and last but not least offers presentation guidelines and techniques.

The remarks and advice from expert designers and educators are extremely helpful in answering questions one might have about the merits of digital versus traditional portfolios, and what designers, producers and educators are looking for in portfolios presented to them by prospective employees and students.

The specifications for constructing a portfolio have not changed all that much: produced work in the front, class-work in the back, strongest work first, update it regularly, and be prepared to show it *anywhere* still apply. However, the range of choices for presentation has expanded dramatically, offering a designer or technician myriad ways to present themselves and their work. Rafael's book takes one through all the options, and makes it possible to make choices among them. He also includes guidelines for self-evaluation that enable one to objectively assess one's own work, portfolio choices and presentation style.

This book is useful to a wide range of people; students applying to college or graduate school, graduate students looking for jobs, designers aspiring to join a professional organization, teachers seeking university positions, professors applying for tenure, and anyone who has found that that the direction of their life has shifted, or who wishes to make a change.

Rafael's book offers all these people direction and the tools necessary to make portfolio decisions for themselves. He addresses the issue of change; making it clear that portfolios need to be modified depending on the purpose for which they are intended. I was especially impressed by the final chapter in which Rafael urges the reader to make plans and set short term goals, thus leading to the drafting of long range ambitions, and to plan the creation of a portfolio that will aid in the achievement of these objectives.

His belief in the power of a portfolio is absolute and inspiring.

And I, for one, have been inspired. So now, if you'll excuse me, I am finally going to go and update my portfolio.

Kitty Leech

Part I

What Is a Design–Tech Portfolio?

Chapter 1
What Is a Portfolio?

A design–tech portfolio is a well-planned portable case that features problem-solving procedures, appealing conceptions, and key materials related to different projects. These materials are carefully organized so it can serve various functions when presented to others:

1. It can serve as a showcase of the artistry, special skills, personal style, volume of work, and process of a designer or a technician.
2. It can be used as a reference archive where the designer or technician features the processes that led to ingenuous design solutions.
3. It can work as a storybook that emphasizes the individual's history, professional growth, and versatility.

Well-executed portfolios showcase volume of work, process, special skills and personal style. Costume designer Jessica Champagne created storyboards to tell the story (from the costume design point of view) of "The Shakespeare Stealer" by Gary Blackwood (Figure 1.1). She won the 2004 ACTF Barbizon Design Award for Region I. Jessica's layout helped explain her approach, the show's production process, and the realized designs.

Figure 1.1
"The Shakespeare Stealer" portfolio: (a) Page 1: project introduction, cast photograph, and book cover.

Figure 1.1 (cont.)
(b) Page 2 (clockwise): character sketches, including Robert Armin, Thomas Pope, and William Shakespeare; photographs: Pope and Shakespeare, and Shakespeare, Armin, and Hamlet.

Figure 1.1 (cont.)
(c) Page 3 (clockwise): production photographs of character Widge in beige, Queen Elizabeth, Queen Elizabeth's dress on form, and Widge in blue; production sketches of Queen Elizabeth and Widge.

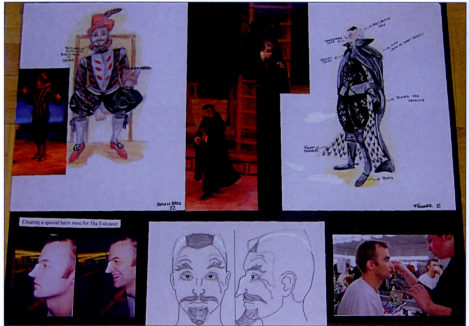

Figure 1.1 (cont.)
(d) Page 4 (clockwise): production photographs of characters Simon Bass and Falconer (full body and half body), Falconer make-up application and nose prosthetic; sketches of Simon Bass plus Falconer's costume and makeup.

THE PORTFOLIO AS A SHOWCASE, REFERENCE ARCHIVE, AND HISTORICAL RECORD

The process of developing and maintaining a design–tech portfolio is not different from the process that takes an idea from a two-dimensional drawing to a three-dimensional product or from an original rendering to a realized production on the theatre stage or set of a film. In order to create an effective showcase, designers and technicians need to plan with this in mind. They need to edit materials and organize layouts in a way that best features their work. Well-executed portfolios can open doors to new opportunities and create winning situations.

THE WINNING DESIGN PORTFOLIO

Each page of the design portfolio tells the story of a specific project. To be effective, each layout has to include a wide range of aspects that speak to the special skills and personal style of the designer, the project resource allocation and budget distribution, and the collaborative process with the director and the company. In the next few pages, we will look at a few sample page choices as a way to introduce us to some effective practices. We will continue to look at more samples and go into more depth in later chapters.

The first sample is a portfolio page for a set designed by Janie Holland. Janie explains: "The photos are from a 'hard' portfolio—by 'hard' portfolio I mean a portfolio with separate pages as opposed to an electronic portfolio. The show is 'Assassins' at the Lyric Stage Company in Boston, directed by Spiro Veloudos. The overall inspiration for the set was an old-fashioned, wooden roller coaster combined with a shooting gallery amusement park booth." Included in her portfolio layout are the paint elevation of the floor (Figure 1.2a) and a photograph from the show (Figure 1.2b). The images are mounted on black mat board.

Figure 1.2
(a) Photograph of Janie Holland's set design for "Assassins" at the Lyric Stage Company in Boston.

**Figure 1.2
(cont.)**
(b) Scenic
portfolio page for
"Assassins."

Sometimes it is important to include research and process on a portfolio page to contextualize a design approach. Costume designer William Henshaw created portfolio pages for the show "American Tragedy: The Case of Clyde Griffith," performed at San Diego State University in 1996. William says: "The premise of this show was that it was yellow journalism; therefore, the renderings were left uncolored and very grainy so as to resemble newsprint and pictures of the 1930s. Preliminary sketches were done all on one page to resemble a layout for a newspaper [see Figure 1.3]. Research for the show was presented on boards to give the feel of a newspaper layout."

Each design discipline has particular aspects of interest, and lighting design is one of the most abstract and difficult to explain visually before a show goes into tech. In a portfolio, good photographs showing clear angles, color fillers, and shadows will help illustrate the special talents and sensibilities of the designer. For "The Idiot," adapted and directed by Alexandre Marine and produced at A.R.T. Institute for Advanced Theater Training in 2004, lighting designer Nicholas Vargelis used white light and sharp angles to add to the high emotional tension in the various scenes. Nicholas' lighting portfolio consists of a series of large (8.5 × 11") photographs, printed on quality photo paper, that reveal his range of design for various plays; each

Figure 1.3
(a) William Henshaw's costume rough-sketch for "American Tragedy."

show is clearly labeled and arranged by scene. The photographs in Figures 1.4a and b are from his portfolio sequence for "The Idiot."

Right after the photographs for "The Idiot," Nicholas showcases his atmospheric and soft lighting for the show "Mud," by Maria Irene Fornes and produced at A.R.T. Institute for Advanced Theater Training in 2003 (Figures 1.4c and d).

Figure 1.3 (cont.)
(b) William Henshaw's final costume design page for "American Tragedy."

The Idiot adapted and directed by Alexandre Marine; General Epanchin's gift to Nastasia.
Scenic: Caleb Wertenbaker; Lighting: Nicholas Vargelis
A.R.T. Institute for Advanced Theater Training 6/2004

Figure 1.4
(a) Lighting by Nicholas Vargelis for "The Idiot"; scene, General Epachin's gift to Nastasia.

The Idiot adapted and directed by Alexandre Marine; Rogojin meets Nastasia Philipovna.
Scenic: Caleb Wertenbaker; Lighting: Nicholas Vargelis
A.R.T. Institute for Advanced Theater Training 6/2004

Figure 1.4 (cont.)
(b) Lighting by Nicholas Vargelis for "The Idiot"; scene, Rogojin meets Nastasia Philipovna.

Figure 1.4 (cont.)
(c) Nicholas Varguelis' lighting design portfolio pages (showing contrast) for "Mud"; scene 1-6, The Starfish.

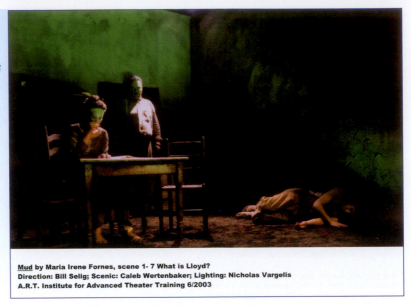

Mud by Maria Irene Fornes, scene 1- 7 What is Lloyd?
Direction: Bill Selig; Scenic: Caleb Wertenbaker; Lighting: Nicholas Vargelis
A.R.T. Institute for Advanced Theater Training 6/2003

Anthony Phelps is a set and lighting designer. He holds an M.F.A. in Design from Minnesota State University, Mankato. His professional memberships include United Scenic Artists, I.A.T.S.E., and USITT. His portfolio contains what I call a classical (some would define it as more traditional) approach that proves very effective for his personal style (Figure 1.5).

Figure 1.4 (cont.)
(d) Nicholas Varguelis' lighting design portfolio pages (showing contrast) for "Mud"; Scene 1-7, What Is Lloyd?

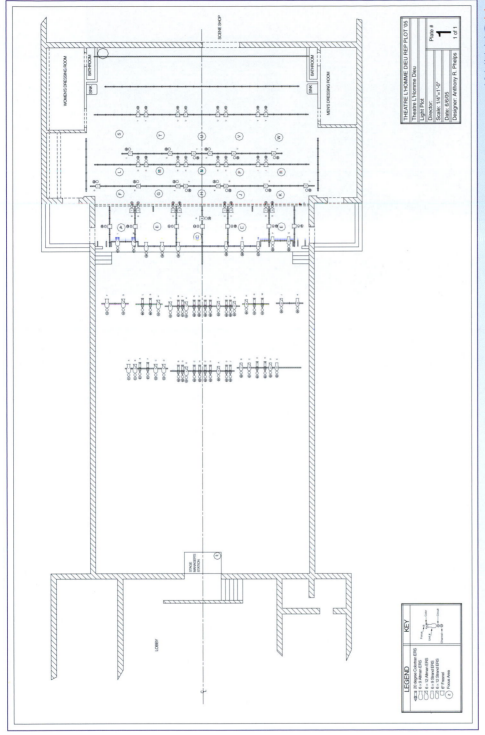

Figure 1.5
(a) Anthony Phelps' full light plot for Theatre L'Homme Dieu in 2005.

Figure 1.5 (cont.) (b) Overview of Anthony Phelps' portfolio layout.

For a sound design portfolio, designer Andy Lewis recommends including block diagram samples of sound systems for shows—one, two, or more, depending on the show: "This is the most visual that a sound design portfolio often gets. It has the benefit of being very obvious in what it is, even to a non-technical producer" (see Figure 1.6).

■ THE WINNING TECHNICAL PORTFOLIO

Just like the design portfolio, the technical portfolio tells the story of a project but with an emphasis on the technical aspects. An effective layout includes a wide range of components, such as technical drawings, budget allocations, engineering solutions, or manufacturing processes. The goal is to feature the special skills and collaboration abilities of the technician. Sometimes, designers are also technicians when they have to come up with

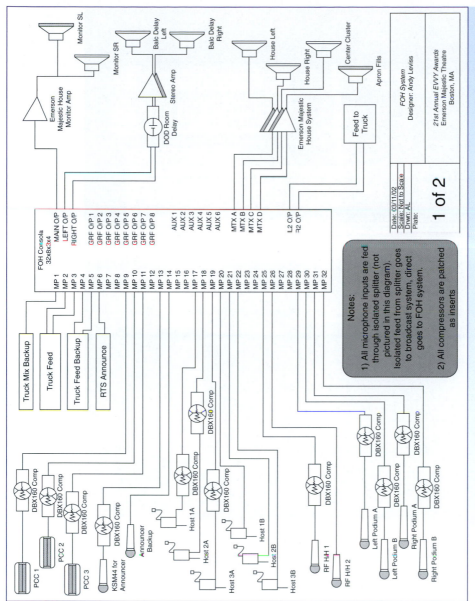

Figure 1.6
Sound designer Andy Lewis' sample block diagram of the sound system for a show.

Figure 1.7
Amanda
Monteiro's
portfolio: (a)
"Thomas of
Woodstock"
medieval shoes;
the portfolio sheet
includes
research,
swatches, project
scope description,
and photographs
of the finished
product.

resourceful solutions to design problems. Costume technician and designer Amanda Monteiro combines samples of build costumes with research, process description and photographs in her portfolio. This gives the reviewer a better idea of her technical expertise as well as her ability to translate design metaphor and period research (Figure 1.7).

Figure 1.7 (cont.) (b) "Under Milkwood" garment construction; the portfolio sheet includes a photocopy of the costume design, swatches, project description, and photographs of the dress form and production.

Now that we have reviewed what the final product may look like in a portfolio, we can ask: How do we develop a new (or existing) portfolio, and how do we maintain it?

Chapter 2

Development Techniques

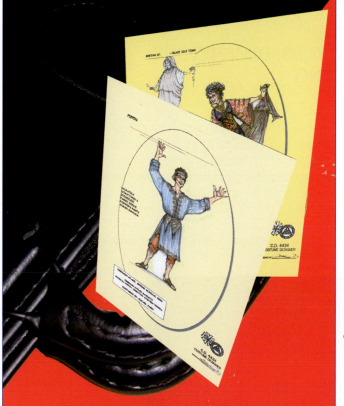

Planning a design–tech portfolio can be a very exciting project. From choosing a carrying case to planning the specific layout of each page, the process gives designers and technicians the opportunity to demonstrate their character, style, talent, and expertise. It can also sometimes be a very large and overwhelming task. This chapter offers some useful information that can assist with the management of this project.

PLANNING AND CREATION

Before investing a lot of time and money in a portfolio, the designer or technician needs to define the goals and uses of the portfolio: Will it be a showcase of artistry and special skills or a reference archive? Will it be used to apply for a job or to apply to a graduate school? Will different parts serve equal or different purposes? Will it be carried on a daily basis or occasionally? Will it hold small documents or large works? How will it be presented? The answers to these questions will serve to clarify the type of case, or cases, to get. For example, if the body of work is very large (in size and volume) and the portfolio is carried only occasionally, then a large case may be the answer. On the other hand, if the work is large but the portfolio case needs to

Figure 2.1
(a) A three-ring binder, which is a very basic portfolio that can be used to apply to an undergraduate program. (Photograph by Eric Cornell.)

travel constantly, then the designer or technician may consider having either a second showcase with reductions of the work or a digital portfolio. Because portfolios come in many styles and sizes (see Figure 2.1), knowing the purpose of a portfolio will help determine the type of case to choose.

MODELS, STYLES, DIMENSIONS, AND HANDLING

Portfolio cases can be grouped into three categories: binders, presentation cases, and folios. Each one of these can be fitted with a variety of sheet holders that can accommodate different projects. Binders are often used for smaller and individual project presentations, cases are more traditional and often favored by designers, and folios are excellent for large, hands-free presentations. When choosing a size, remember that the dimensions given for portfolios, presentation cases, binders, and refill pages are the maximum size of the artwork that can be accommodated, not the outside measurements.

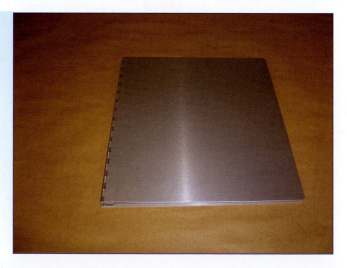

Figure 2.1 (cont.)
(b) An aluminum case, which can be used by technicians working in hard-hat areas. (Photograph by Eric Cornell.)

Figure 2.1 (cont.)
(c) Detail of a classic portfolio leather case with leather handles. (Photograph by Eric Cornell.)

BINDERS

Acid-free sheets are recommended to protect artwork, and reinforced rings are a plus for durability. There are many varieties of binders, so it is important to do some research prior to purchasing a specific model. Some designers and technicians have different binders for different purposes. The following are some examples of the products available in the market today:

1. *Multi-ring binders* can be attractive and sturdy; they usually include 5 to 10 sheet protectors and have a 30- to 50-sheet capacity, depending on the manufacturer. They can be covered in leather, vinyl, or fabric. Binders with metal reinforced corners are sturdier. These binders are ideal for small documents and often-traveling portfolios (Figure 2.2). Typical measurements include 14 × 11″, 17 × 11″, 17 × 14″, 17 × 22″, and 18 × 24″

2. *Easel binders* feature convenient spine-mounted retractable handles and allow a horizontal or vertical presentation. They are ideal for on-the-road presentations and industrial designs. They often include 10 sheet protectors and have a 30-sheet capacity. They can be found in 17 × 14″, 11 × 8.5″, 14 × 11″, and 24 × 18″ sheet sizes.

Figure 2.2
17 × 11″ Multi-ring binder; this portfolio is useful for carrying sketches to meetings or spec sessions in a shop. The costume sketches shown here for the musical "Pippin" were done in 2004 by this book's author for Emerson Stage. (The sketches were featured in the *Entertainment Design Magazine*, ED Designer Sketches Book feature, June 2004.)

Figure 2.3
(a) Slide-in binder case, which opens as a folder and has an elastic clasp at the top.

3. *Aluminum portfolio binders* are stylish and durable, ideal for carpentry, rigging, and electrics (see Figure 2.1b). They usually include 10 archival multi-ring sheet protectors, a zippered black nylon jacket, and a set of screw-post extensions. Sizes include 11 × 8.5″, 14 × 11″, and 17 × 11″.

4. *Slide-in pocket page binders* are great for work that should be included with the main portfolio, but they can also stand on their own (*i.e.*, specific period research and specialty craft projects; see Figures 2.3a and b). They have clear pocket-type pages for an organized, stylish, and professional presentation. This type of portfolio is ideal for individual project presentations and usually contains 24 pocket pages with black inserts. The best are acid and PVC free. Sizes vary depending on the manufacturer, but they generally come in 8.5 × 11″, 9 × 12″, 11 × 14″, and 14 × 17″ sizes.

5. *Standard three-ring binders* are general-use binders for letter (8.5 × 11″), legal (11 × 14″), and ledger (11 × 17″) sheet sizes. It is best if they have interior storage pockets for miscellaneous items. The depth of these binders can vary from 1 to 3 inches. They are ideal for storing organizational data, charts, slides, photographs, and research (Figure 2.3c).

There are many varieties of binders; the desired function (work storage or presentation) will determine the best choice.

Figure 2.3 (cont.)
(b) Slide-in pocket page sheets with group costume sketches designed in 2005 by this book's author for Opera Boston's "Alceste." This type of binder case is great for carrying sketches to design and production meetings.

Figure 2.3 (cont.) (c) Standard three-ring binder with clear tab dividers, which are ideal for holding and presenting such paperwork as budgets, construction specs, or Q sheets.

|PRESENTATION CASES AND FOLIOS

Presentation cases and folios can serve multiple purposes. They can be the main portfolio cases, holding all the paperwork for a project, or they can be (depending on size) presentation aids used at production meeting presentations.

■ Presentation Cases

Presentation cases are the most often used portfolios in the design–tech field and can be found in many styles with covers ranging from durable vinyl to metal to soft leather. Many of the varieties found in the market today feature a solid construction (reinforced base, metal protective floor bumpers, and industrial-strength zippers) and include inside pockets and carrying handles, further adding to their manageability and multifunctionality. Some cases even feature multiple-use pockets in their interior for the storage of accessories, such as computer disks or business cards. The sheets in this type of portfolio can be permanent parts of the carrying mechanism or can be removable inserts in multi-ring books (Figure 2.4). This feature is especially important for someone who may have various books but can only afford one case. Most presentation cases include 10 standard archival sheet protectors and have a 25- to 30-sheet capacity. They measure 11 × 8.5", 14 × 11", 17 × 14", 22 × 17", and 24 × 18".

■ Folios

Folios are great for hands-free presentations involving, for example, industrial designs and museum installations. These are some recommended styles:

1. *Easel folios*—This type of portfolio is designed with an integrated easel stand, which allows easy desktop display. For standard book use and storage, the easel

Figure 2.4
(a) Leather
presentation case.

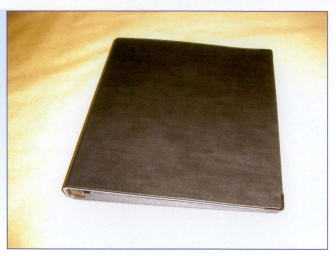

folds away. Covers are often made of durable black polypropylene. They can hold as many as 20 pages. Acid-free and PVC-free pages are best. Usual sizes are 8.5 × 11″, 11 × 14″, and 14 × 17″ (Figure 2.5).

2. *Oversized expandable portfolios*—For large works, these extra-large capacity portfolios hold up to 25 sheets of 3/16-inch foamboard. Zippers open to allow the portfolio to lie flat. This type of portfolio often includes two 10 × 13″ outside zipper pockets, a business card window, two side handles, and a 6-inch expandable gusset. Some have an optional detachable wheel-board for easy transport of heavy artwork. They can expand from 25 × 37 × 6″ to 41 × 61 × 6″.

As we can see, there are many presentation cases and folios on the market, and they can serve multiple purposes. They can be the main portfolio cases, holding all the paperwork for a project, or they can be presentation aids used at production meeting presentations.

Figure 2.4 (cont.)
(b) Presentation case; the costume sketches shown here for the musical "Pippin" were done in 2004 by this book's author for Emerson Stage. (The sketches were featured in the *Entertainment Design Magazine*, ED Designer Sketches Book feature, June 2004.)

Figure 2.5
(a) Easel folio with twill fabric tape closures.

INSIDE THE CASE: SUPPLIES AND MATERIALS

The portfolio is not just a carrying case, of course; organization of the contents inside of it is just as important. The proper sheet holders will add to the overall look of a presentation, the manageability of the display sheets will aid in the handling of materials, and the durability of the materials will ensure that you have a healthy and long-lasting showcase.

MULTI-RING REFILL PAGES

1. *Laser archival*—These are high-quality, super-clear, nonstick, polypropylene sheet protectors that prevent color alteration and transfer. They are highly recommended for digital images. They are often sealed on three sides with a reinforced, perforated, multi-ring binder edge and contain acid-free black paper inserts. Sizes vary from 8-1/2 × 11″ to 18″ × 24″.

Figure 2.5 (cont.)
(b) Easel folios are great for hands-on and table spread presentations; sketches and paperwork can be stored but are free for handling.

2. *Clear polyester archival*—These clear polyester sheets often come with deluxe acid-free black paper inserts and standard multi-ring perforations. They are recommended for digital images and for all laser copies, as well, and will not lift print or toner off artwork. Sizes vary from 8-1/2 × 11″ to 18″ × 24″.
3. *Polypropylene archival*—These are heavy-duty, welded, polypropylene multi-ring sheet protectors of archival quality (.0045 polypropylene). They are unplasticized, heat resistant, and chemically stable. They come with acid- and lignin-free black paper inserts. Both plastic and paper pass the photographic activity test (PAT) and meet all ANSI requirements for archival storage. Sizes vary from 8-1/2 × 11″ to 11″ × 17″.

THREE-RING BINDER SHEET PROTECTORS

1. *Sheet protectors*—When using a standard three-ring binder, the best top load sheet protectors are manufactured of heavyweight polypropylene for crystal clear clarity, safety, and extra strength. They are sealed on three sides and contain pre-punched holes for standard three-ring binders. They come in different varieties, such as top loading; side loading, quick load (two sides are open), and fold-out sheets. Page sizes include letter (8-1/2 × 11″), legal (11 × 14″), and ledger (11 × 17″) (Figures 2.6a and b).
2. *Storage pages*—For photograph/slide archival purposes, 4-mil polypropylene pages are recommended; they provide high clarity for superior presentation and are suitable for long-term storage. They can be used with standard three-ring binders and are PVC-free. They can be bought in packages of 25 pages. They are designed to hold 2 × 2″, 3.5 × 5″, 4 × 5″, 4 × 6″, 4 × 7″, 4 × 11″, 5 × 7″, and 8 × 10″ slides or photographs.
3. *Tab-dividers*—Dividers are useful for separating projects by sections and by categories. They come with clear tabs and blank white inserts. They can be found in traditional 8-tab packs or big-tab 5-tab packs, for which the inserts provide 50% more printing area for tab titles than traditional tab inserts. The tab inserts can be printed using an inkjet or laser printer (Figure 2.6c).

Many portfolio refill pages and sheet protector options designed for a variety of uses are available on the market. The right choice can add pizzazz to a portfolio presentation.

Figure 2.6
(a) Sheet holders come in many varieties. Quick-load sheet holders are very practical when paperwork must be removed and stored repeatedly.

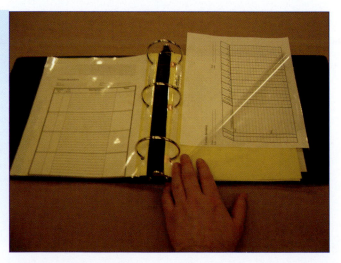

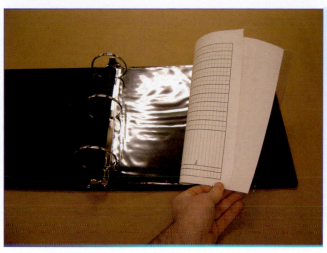

Figure 2.6 (cont.)
(b) The 11 × 17″ ledger-size, fold-out sheets holders are very practical for larger documents, charts, CAD printouts, etc.

SPECIALTY LAYOUT MATERIALS AND SUPPLIES

The materials and supplies needed to put a portfolio together and create the desire layout include sheet protectors, tab dividers, résumé paper, matboards, double-sided tape, paper-cutting gadgets, computer printouts, labels, etc. The following are some important aspects to consider when choosing these materials:

1. *Durability*—The best material choices are acid free, PVC free, and heat resistant to preserve the work and to prevent lifting or transferring the color onto the sheet holders.
2. *Safety*—When using paper-cutting gadgets, it is important to observe the manufacturer's instructions and to be comfortable using the equipment in order to avoid personal injuries and damaging one's work.
3. *Legibility*—Background paper, matboards, labels, and résumé papers should not compete with or detract from the project information on display. When choosing any of these it is also important to take into consideration that the paper will have to be photocopied and the work has to be legible in these copies.
4. *Versatility*—Depending on the complexity of the project and how many components will be on display, the materials chosen must allow flexibility in the pres-

Figure 2.6 (cont.)
(c) Tab dividers aid in separating parts of a project and categorizing and organizing paperwork.

entation: Is the project going to be taken out of its sheet holders? Does the project have multiple components that require different portfolio cases? Does the project include small inserts such as reviews, program, etc., that may not require full large pages? Do all of the components have to be bound, or should some be free for handling purposes?

WHERE TO FIND SPECIALTY MATERIALS AND SUPPLIES

Larger cities may give the designer or technician the option to visit an art store in person and speak to an informed salesperson, if necessary. When this is not an option because of geographical location or a busy schedule, the Internet is the best way to access a very diverse market with many products. Experience suggests that it is best to research first and shop second. Sometimes, after identifying a source online, it might be a good idea for a designer or technician to call the company's customer service number to ask questions about their products directly. These are some companies available online (in alphabetical order):

1. AllArtSupply.com (http://www.artresource.com/portfolio_cases.html)—Portfolio cases and carrying devices
2. Charrette (https://www.charrette.com)—Art supplies as well as portfolio cases, folios, and archival sheets
3. Colours Artist Supplies (http://www.artistsupplies.com; located in Canada)
4. Dick Blick (http://www.dickblick.com)—Art supplies as well as portfolio cases, folios, and archival sheets
5. Digital Art Supplies (http://www.digitalartsupplies.com)
6. Madison Art Shopping (http://www.madisonartshop.com)
7. Office Depot (http://www.officedepot.com)—Office supplies and layout materials
8. Pearl Fine Art Supplies (http://www.pearlpaint.com)
9. Portfolios-and-Art-Cases (http://www.portfolios-and-art-cases.com)—All kinds of portfolio cases and hard-to-find sizes
10. Rex Art (http://www.rexart.com)
11. Staples (http://www.staples.com)—Basic three-ring binders, standard sheet protectors, office supplies, labels, etc.
12. Utrech Art (http://www.utrechtart.com)

Remember that there are many art stores on the Internet, and sometimes if a deal seems too good to be true, it probably is. Check your local Yellow Page listings for close-by retailers and the Internet for specials and discounts in different stores. If you are on a deadline and need specialty items, do not rely only on the Internet to get them; it is always best to call a store's customer service to check on stock availability, product specifics, and delivery times. Sometimes stores will refer callers to another vendor that may carry something more suitable to their needs. Always research first!

LAYOUT TECHNIQUES

Well-organized portfolios showcase projects in logical, clear, and entertaining sequences. Each sheet should hold key information; planning the sequences and layout will help determine the type of portfolio case to use and the type of sheet holders or refills to get. Some of the basic aspects to consider when planning the structure of a portfolio are reviewed in more detail in Chapter 9 (which includes samples). At this point, we are only focusing on the initial plan or strategy that will help us get the right materials.

BASIC STRATEGY TO GET THE RIGHT MATERIALS

In order to make these choices we first need to consider the opening page of the portfolio and the layout or visual organization of the portfolio, as well as conversation pieces and the back pocket:

- *How to begin*—The opening page serves as an introduction to the designer or technician and also an introduction to the work featured in the portfolio. It needs to be clear and direct; it sets the stage of the presentation. It can be as simple as an identification page or a place to hold a Résumé.
- *Layout plan, or how to tell the project's story*—Related pages should maintain the same layout direction to guide the eye of the viewer. It is best to avoid displaying different projects next to each other, so there is no confusion with regard to what the reviewer is looking at. Planning project breaks can help determine how many pages to get for a portfolio. Remember that all projects must be clearly labeled and properly keyed. Is best to display the work in sequences that include design ideas first, photos of process second, and final product last.
- *Conversation pieces*—In order to create interest, smaller sheets can be added within a project. These smaller sheets can hold photographs, newspaper articles, research, etc. Foldout pages can be added to present smaller components of a presentation in order to create interest—like a "play within the play." Always make sure that these smaller sheets are compatible with the portfolio case to be used. The goal is to add an element of surprise, variety, and flexibility to the display.
- *Back pocket*—The back pocket includes extra materials that might be of interest to some of the reviewers. These are materials that can be used to inform process or add clarity to a project; for example: a costume designer who has worked as a wardrobe supervisor may have costume quick-change plots to present to a production manager. Sometimes a simple three-ring binder can contain all back pocket support materials.

In this chapter, we have established some foundations and goals. We now have information that can help us choose a portfolio case, and we have information that can help us begin to gather some necessary supplies. Next, we have to answer these questions: How do we pick the work to be featured in the portfolio? How do we develop an effective showcase?

WORKBOOK: PLANNING AND CREATION

WHAT CARRYING AND DISPLAY MATERIALS
WOULD I LIKE TO USE TO PUT TOGETHER A
PORTFOLIO?

Chapter 3
The Effective Showcase

In previous chapters, we have established that a portfolio is (1) a showcase for the artistry of a designer and a technician, (2) a reference archive that features processes and design solutions, and (3) a storybook that emphasizes the individual's professional growth and versatility. In this chapter, we are going to explore using the portfolio as a marketing tool to achieve specific goals.

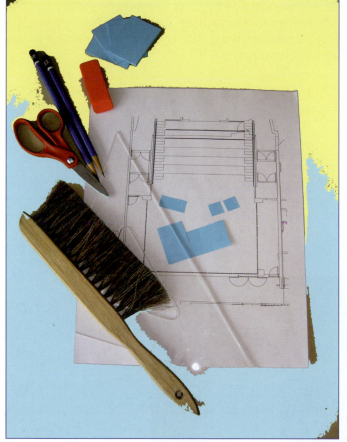

GENERAL CONSIDERATIONS

The audience that it is intended for can define a portfolio. A portfolio used to apply for graduate school may be different from a portfolio used to get a professional design job; a portfolio used to apply for a technical job may differ from one used by a designer. Each goal will have a different set of variables that the individual must consider. To assemble an effective portfolio, it is important to get information regarding what the portfolio reviewer will be looking for and to plan accordingly. When the potential uses of the portfolio have been defined, the next step is to plan the organization—beginning, middle, and end—of the work to be displayed. The order and display of the various parts should be well thought out so the portfolio contains comprehensive materials and communicates clearly. Determining the goal of the portfolio will help with choosing the most appropriate work and layout materials.

ORGANIZING THE BODY OF WORK: BEGINNING, MIDDLE, AND END

THE BEGINNING

The beginning refers to the introductory page of the portfolio. It may be a résumé, an identification page, an opening title page, a table of contents, etc. The identification page is especially important if your portfolio is being reviewed when you are not in the room; for example, some colleges review portfolios without the applicants being present. Some designers and technicians prefer a portfolio that has a front pocket so they can store a résumé, brochure, or other similar items in it.

Julianne Tavares was one of my students. She earned a B.F.A. degree in Design–Technology at Emerson College in 2005. Her concentration was Set Design and Scenic Charge/Painter. During her senior portfolio review, she presented a very well-organized portfolio that helps illustrate some of the points addressed in this chapter (Figure 3.1).

THE MIDDLE

The middle of a portfolio contains the work of the designer or technician and is organized by project. It should be versatile and support the goals of the portfolio. It is best to organize each project with its own beginning, middle, and end to help tell the story. The layout should include sketches, photographs of models (or other three-dimensional items created for the produc-

Figure 3.1
(a) Julianne Tavares' portfolio opening page holds her résumé and business card.

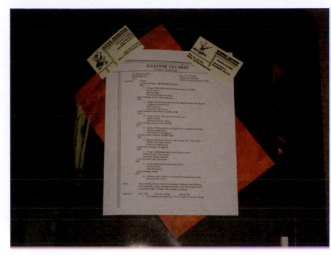

Figure 3.1 (cont.)
(b) Julianne Tavares portfolio opening page detail; notice that her sense of color and composition makes a statement about her personality. This type of opening or identification page (with a résumé) would be very helpful if she applies for a MFA program and is not in the room when the reviewers critique her portfolio.

tion), and photographs of the realized project. It is also helpful to include programs, reviews, and some process photographs. In some cases, when the portfolio has multiple purposes, it is important to separate projects with title pages or to tab the different parts (Figure 3.2).

Typical subdivisions (by category) of the middle body of the portfolio include:

- *Venue*—Traditional venues such as theatre, television, film, and video, as well as allied fields and newer venues such as industrials, concerts, art installations, museum installations, and virtual productions.
- *Production*—Musical theatre, children's theatre, music video, industrial design, Shakespearean drama, dance theatre, virtual scenery, novelty or theme parks, comedy, or commercials.
- *Type of work*—Produced shows, class projects, conceptual projects, design and technical projects, allied fields, installations, or exhibits.

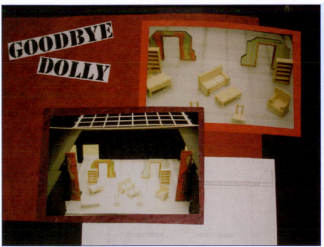

Figure 3.2
(a) Julianne Tavares' page layout includes photographs of models in addition to the fully realized set.

Figure 3.2 (cont.)
(b) Julianne's Tavares' full set photograph; notice how her model reflects in the realized product.

| THE END

The end could be either the last section of a project display (Figure 3.3a) or the end of the portfolio itself. The layout of the last section of a project should include details that best feature the individual's contributions to that project (Figure 3.3b). The last pages of the portfolio should include one or various smaller projects for which the presenter particularly wants to be remembered. The back pocket is also found at the end of the portfolio but is not necessarily featured. It holds various samples of reference and support materials that can be used to show other aspects of the projects (e.g., extra sketches, samples of drafting, budget specs, flowcharts).

Figure 3.2 (cont.)
(c) Proper labels and keys with important show information, such as the name of the play, venue, sketch detail, etc. They are necessary to help inform the reviewers (and the presenter).

Figure 3.3
(a) Close-up of Julianne Tavares' portfolio page showing a show portal design that she painted.

BEST ARTWORK, MEDIA REVIEWS, AND PHOTOGRAPHS TO FEATURE

Reviewers are critics accustomed to seeing many portfolios. They will have many questions and high expectations. Featured artwork must be clearly labeled, fixed, and organized. Draftings, blueprints, and CAD drawings should be a readable size. Photographs must be true to stage color and contain detail. Research and reference materials should include their sources and titles. Media articles should include dates and title pages. Show programs, reputable production company brochures, and show posters or postcards can be part of the layout and can add status to the presentation. The goal is to give the reviewer as many contexts as possible so they can quickly understand the scale and venue of the work that you are presenting.

Figure 3.3 (cont.)
(b) Julianne Tavares last portfolio page showing the layout for a specific project; here, she includes production photographs next to her drawings.

Karen Perlow has been a freelance lighting designer since 1986. She is an instructor at the Massachusetts Institute of Technology and was a 2003 IRNE winner for best lighting design. In her portfolio she includes sequences of large photographs that clearly demonstrate a wide range of design ideas executed for each of her shows (Figures 3.4a–f) For some scenes, Karen needed to create an expansive sense of space; in others, an intimate feeling while accommodating different upstage playing spaces. In each photograph, the composition creates a sense of environment and mood and integrates the playing areas and coordinating color palettes.

BACK POCKET: RESEARCH AND ORGANIZATIONAL PAPERWORK

There will always be materials that seem superfluous, and some productions will have more sketches and graphics than others. If a project has a lot of material that the designer deems important, it can be saved in the portfolio back pocket. The back pocket usually contains reference materials—such as extra research, technical information, photographs, or design and technical solutions—of specific projects that did not fit or could not be featured within the main body of the work. The materials in the back pocket should also be organized and labeled clearly. They can be used as conversation pieces if the interviewer wants more information about a specific project or skill. If the designer or technician has a large body of work, the back pocket (like the portfolio) will only include highlights of archival materials. These archival materials should be cataloged and filed properly so they can be used (if called upon) for installations featuring samples for educational, marketing, or exhibition purposes.

THE DESIGNER AND TECHNICIAN'S ARCHIVES

As the years go by and samples accumulate, it is important to file and catalog different projects. In the academic world, these files can be used to attain promotions or tenure; elsewhere, they can be used as teaching tools or reference materials, can become the basis for articles for a magazine, or can be used at artist retrospective exhibits and installations. To illustrate this aspect of portfolio archiving, I reached out to my former classmate and colleague John Iacovelli; he is an accomplished, award-winning designer who has many nominations and an Emmy Award to his name.

Iacovelli has done theatrical set designs for Broadway and regional theatre productions, art direction and production design for television and film, and art direction and production design for videos and industrials. Some of his impressive career credits include set design for many Broadway productions (*e.g.*, "Peter Pan"), art direction for such television shows as "The Crosby Show," production design for "Resurrection Boulevard" and "Babylon 5," art direction for the film "Honey I Shrunk the Kids," and industrial installations for the Summer 1996 Olympics and Disney. The 2004 USITT

Figure 3.4
(a–c) Scenes from "A Little Night Music" produced at the Lyric Stage Company of Boston in 2004 (director, Spiro Veloudos; scenic design, Christina Todesco; costume design, David Cabral; light design, Karen Perlow).

Figure 3.4 (cont.)

(d) Scene from "City of Angels" produced at the Boston Conservatory of Music in 2005 (director, Paul Daigneault; scenic design, Crystal Tiala; costume design, Stacey Stevens; light design, Karen Perlow).

Figure 3.4 (cont.)

(e) Scene from "Company" produced by the SpeakEasy Stage Company in 2004 (director, Paul Daigneault; scenic design, Eric Levenson; costume design, Gail A. Buckley; light design, Karen Perlow).

Figure 3.4 (cont.)

(f) Scene from "Scapin" produced by the New Repertory Theatre in 2004 (director, Rick Lombardo; scenic design, Janie Howland; costume design, Francis McSherry; light design, Karen Perlow).

Figure 3.5
(a) Iacovelli's exhibit, USITT Design Expo 2004: wall sketch display.

Design Expo featured Iacovelli's work. The display included his recent work for theatre, television, and film. He organized his archival materials to show process, samples, and final designs; he had a beginning, middle, and end; and he demonstrated that portfolio archives can be traveling installations (Figures 3.5a–g).

Figure 3.5 (cont.)
(b) Iacovelli's exhibit, USITT Design Expo 2004: design plans and an actual set piece.

**Figure 3.5
(cont.)**
(c) Iacovelli's
exhibit, USITT
Design Expo 2004:
set models wall.

MARKETING AND NETWORKING: IDENTIFYING PORTFOLIO REQUIREMENTS BY VENUE

In this section, the focus is on college application procedures, higher education organizations that offer specialized services and scholarships, institutes, and unions. Before pursuing any venue it is of the utmost importance for individuals to do in-depth research about the best opportunities available for their specific levels of skills and temperaments. Some requirements are universal and some are specific to the venue.

**Figure 3.5
(cont.)**
(d) Iacovelli's
exhibit, USITT
Design Expo 2004:
his Emmy Award,
a recognition of
his artistry and
fantastic body of
work.

Figure 3.5 (cont.)
(e) Iacovelli's exhibit, USITT Design Expo 2004: set for the television show "Ed" (produced by NBC/Viacom).

Figure 3.5 (cont.)
(f–g) Iacovelli's exhibit, USITT Design Expo 2004: details from "Vincent in Brixton" (producer, The Pasadena Playhouse; director, Elina deSantos; scenery design, John Iacovelli; costume designer, Maggie Morgan; lighting design, Leigh Allen).

COLLEGE APPLICATION

Portfolio requirements will vary depending on the program that the student is applying for. Undergraduate programs may place more emphasis on the applicant's artwork and general theatrical experience, while graduate programs tend to look for more area-specific and in-depth production work experience. When planning a portfolio to apply for college, it is important to obtain the specific requirements of each school. Most of them will conduct reviews without the applicant present, and most colleges will be looking for examples of artwork, nonrealized projects, and realized production work. Usually, the artwork requirements will include providing samples, such as drawings, paintings, models, or sculptures. Photographs of such artwork can be submitted in place of the originals; the scale of the project should be noted on each project to help differentiate the scale of it (e.g., a large mural *versus* a postcard).

Samples of theatrical projects can include rough and final sketches; material samples and swatches; blueprints, draftings, or CAD samples; models or photographs of models; light plots and Q sheets; production photographs; etc. Some colleges will ask for a digital portfolio (samples provided on a CD), while others will require an actual portfolio (which will include a self-addressed return envelope). Each design–tech area will focus on specific samples. The area of scenic design often requires scale models (or photographs), scale ground plans and sections, and examples of architectural sketches (e.g., furniture, interior details); it is important to organize these samples by script or play. The area of costume design often requires sketches with fabric swatches, period research, and technical detail drawings. Concept plates, fashion cut sheets, and samples of built garments may be required, as well; again, it is important to organize these samples by script or play. The area of lighting design light often requires concept statements about ideas for the projects presented and their execution, as well as inspirational photographs, research, or color drawings. It also requires a plot (computer and drafting), full paperwork, and production photographs. Here, too, it is important to organize these samples by script or play.

A successful portfolio will be as versatile as possible. It should contain materials that display multiple skills, the work should be properly labeled, and the presentation should be well organized and clear. Such a portfolio can be presented at higher education organizations and other groups that offer professional reviews, scholarships, internships, competitions, or professional job placements that will enhance the experience of the participants. There are many of these venues and they all have websites with updated comprehensive guidelines, clear information, and application procedures. Some organizations worth researching are the University/Resident Theatre Association (U/RTA), the Southeastern Theatre Conference (SETC), the New England Theatre Conference (NETC), the United States Institute for Theatre Technology (USITT), and Chapter 829 of United Scenic Artists (USA). The choice as to which one of these venues to pursue depends on level of skill, location, finances, membership restrictions, etc. It is important to research them thoroughly before making a decision.

ORGANIZATIONS THAT OFFER PORTFOLIO REVIEWS

The following summary provides general information about different higher education organizations and associated groups that offer portfolio reviews as part of their services and membership privileges.

U/RTA (http://www.urta.com)

The University/Resident Theatre Association is the largest consortium of professional companies and educational theatre programs in the United States. It offers a variety of services to members and nonmembers, including students, theatre professionals, and producing companies, and facilitates access to graduate college scholarships and jobs with professional theatre companies. After following application procedures, paying an application fee, and scheduling a portfolio review, applicants receive support materials that include a copy of the *Directory of Theatre Training Programs* (complete listing of U/RTA member schools and services) and the indispensable *Guidelines for Portfolio Presentation and Interview Procedures*. The *Guidelines* booklet provides answers for many questions related to setting up and organizing the portfolio for review. The requirements are similar to those listed earlier in the college application section.

SETC (http://www.setc.org)

The Southeastern Theatre Conference is one of the largest and most active regional theatre organizations in the country. It is open to a national audience, and it focuses on providing theatre experiences of the highest possible standards. Schools must be an institutional member for students to enter the conference. SETC offers design professional critiques at design competitions at both undergraduate and graduate levels. Adjudicators are well known, highly acclaimed designers. Specific details for entry can be found at the SETC website under Student Guidelines. Scene Design Award minimum requirements include a ground plan in specific scale, color sketch, model, and/or painter's elevations, plus a statement of the designer's approach. Other items to include are research materials; preliminary sketches; full drafting package, including ground plan, elevations, section, and detail drawings; and photographs, if realized. The Costume Design Award minimum requirements include color costume sketches (each sketch must be swatched), statement of the approach to the design, research materials, preliminary sketches, a costume plot, and photographs, if realized. The Lighting Design Award minimum requirements include light plot drawn using USITT standard symbols, in addition to dimmer/control schedule, magic sheets, instrument schedule, hanging section (scenic designer's is acceptable), photographs of realized production (graduate level), and a statement of the approach to the design. Other materials include research materials, preliminary sketches, cue sheets, and storyboards.

NETC (http://www.netconline.org)

The New England Theatre Conference is an organization dedicated to providing its members with professional services, career development, and playwright recognition awards in the theatre arts. It serves Connecticut, Maine, Massachusetts, New Hampshire, Rhode Island, and Vermont. NETC conducts theatre auditions annually for positions in summer and year-round professional theatres. Positions include actors, singers, dancers, designers, technicians, and production staff. The participating companies include Equity and non-Equity summer stock, Shakespearean and Renaissance festivals, musical theatre, children's theatre, revues, and many others. Tech and staff interviews are conducted to fill the many positions available in these fields. Every applicant receives a complete list of all participating producers and their season, and every producer receives the résumé of every applicant. Membership is required.

USITT (http://www.usitt.org)

The United States Institute for Theatre Technology, Inc., is an association of design, production, and technology professionals in the performing arts and entertainment industry. USITT promotes advancement and development of the knowledge and skills of its members by sharing information about new technologies, research, and educational programs, as well as safety, industry standards, and ethical practices; in addition, it sponsors exhibits and conferences and provides networking opportunities. Various committees of the organization recommend potential award, grant, and fellowship recipients. During their yearly conference and stage expo, USITT offers special in-depth review sessions for individuals to discuss their portfolios, résumés, and careers with professionals in specific areas. These sessions are open to undergraduate, graduate, and working designers and technicians. They last 30 minutes and are facilitated by professional volunteer members from various disciplines.

USA CHAPTER 829 AND IATSE (http://www.usa829.org; http://www.iatse-intl.org/index_flash.html)

United Scenic Artists and the International Alliance of Theatrical Stage Employees (IATSE), Moving Pictures Technicians, Artists, and Allied Crafts of the United States, Its Territories, and Canada are both labor unions representing technicians, artisans, and craftspeople in the entertainment industry, including live theatre, motion pictures, television production, and trade shows. Membership provides many benefits, including retirement plans, credit unions, health benefits, etc. Becoming a member of USA is a rigorous process and requires various types of exams. The TRACK A exam is for designers with at least three years of professional, not academic, experience. The exam is a 20-minute interview, during which time various judges review the applicant's portfolio and some required samples. Applicants who fail to be recommended after this interview may consider the TRACK B open exam or the apprenticeship program. It is advisable for applicants to do everything possible to present their portfolios in such a way that the judges will be able to assess the candidate's range of knowledge, experience, and qualifications. The panel consists of six designers and the interview lasts 20 minutes. Flat-table presentations are favored for easy handling of materials. Portfolios should include main project documentation (as prescribed in the application for each discipline), rough drawings/sketches, models, color renderings, complete draftings, storyboards, location photographs, research or reference materials, production photographs, and videotapes. The IATSE website notes that: "It's much better to have all the documentation for 1 or 2 projects than bits and pieces of two dozen projects." Depending on time, judges may also be interested in assessing organizational skills and flexibility, which they can evaluate by viewing production paperwork, such as show bibles, organizational paperwork, budgets (whenever possible), Polaroids, and shopping lists.

In this chapter, we have explored some portfolio development and organization techniques, plus networking and marketing venues. Next: What does the final product begin to look like? What do experts in the field recommend?

WORKBOOK: BEGINNING, MIDDLE, AND END
LIST PROJECTS THAT YOU WOULD LIKE TO
FEATURE IN THE BEGINNING, MIDDLE, AND END
OF YOUR PORTFOLIO.

Chapter 4
Types of Portfolios

In October 2004, *Entertainment Design* magazine featured an article called "Avoiding a Portfolio Imbroglio." Mark Newman—the magazine's managing editor—conducted interviews and wrote this very comprehensive article, paying careful attention to the expectations described by various design-technology experts about different types of portfolios. The comments included in his article help illustrate what reviewers in different areas of concentration look for and respond best to. This chapter will include Mr. Newman's findings, plus feedback and samples from colleagues who contributed to this book.

Avoiding a Portfolio Imbroglio

by Mark A. Newman

Entertainment Design, October 1, 2004

"Who am I anyway? Am I my résumé?" so goes the lyric from the opening number of "A Chorus Line" sung by an aspiring triple-threat. For aspiring theatre designers, the answer to the lyric is yes . . . and no. Design faculty at top colleges can easily see through the gloss of a slick portfolio. An attractive presentation is nice, but if the talent and the ability are not there, the presentation is moot.

In the Fall 2004 issue of the *U/RTA Update*, U/RTA executive director Scott Steele noted that portfolios are partly about concealing weaknesses. But a designer's strengths should not be buried for the sake of presentation. A portfolio that is all "bells and whistles" keeps university design recruiters from seeing what really exists in the student's mind, what gifts the students truly have, or even where the real talent deficits may hide.

Know How

For example, if you cannot adequately represent your designs by taking pencil to paper, you already have an uphill battle. "I'm looking for art skills, traditionally called 'visual arts,' which is problematic in the American educational system in terms of training designers," says Richard Isackes, chair at the University of Texas, Austin, and a set designer. "Most candidates have been theatre majors in their institutions, which seems completely appropriate but the skills of a theatre designer really start with skills of a visual artist." He added that some of the best designers he has seen have come out of architectural programs.

"Far and away the most important skill to me is drawing," Isackes continues. "Drawing is a learned skill. It is not a skill that I can teach at the beginning of a graduate training program along with all the other things that need to be taught in terms of learning how to design for performance."

Isackes is particularly interested in students who have adequate experience in figure drawing because he believes that is where one really learns to draw. "A basic understanding of perspective, drafting, and two- and three-dimensional work is also essential," he says. "There are fundamental classes that are taught in most college art departments where they can get these skills. If they know how to draw, I can teach them how to make a model; I can't teach them if they don't have basic skills."

Drawing is also imperative from a lighting design point of view, especially examples of hand drafting, which should not be ignored just because computer drafting is available. "You can't be a lighting designer without the ability to hand-draft," says Bill Teague, a professor of theatre at the University of Alabama who teaches both lighting and technical theatre design. "It's a skill you just have to have. You can hire someone to do the computer renderings."

Scenic, costume, and lighting designers need to show an impressive command of the visual media, according to Dave Tosti-Lane, chair of the Performance Production Department at Cornish College in Seattle. "They should be able to draw—freehand, not just in Photoshop®—draft, deal with color, and understand color both in light and pigment," he says. "Lighting designers should be able to represent their ideas graphically and be able to communicate a lighting idea to someone who does not speak the language of the designer, which is really the key for all designers: find a way to translate your ideas so that people who think differently than you can understand them."

A student's portfolio should not only present their capabilities but also the direction they hope to pursue. "I don't respond well to a student's portfolio that is so broad that they set themselves out as a jack of all trades, which is not realistic in terms of what the industry is," says Peter Beudert, a set designer and the head of design and technical production at the University of Arizona. "I encourage students to have as much specificity as possible in terms of where they think their strengths are or what they want to work on in grad school. That tends to be one thing that some students don't achieve too well."

The Right Stuff

It is also important to show not only your final work but how you got to that point. "Show process, show process, show process," is Tosti-Lane's mantra. "Don't just show pretty pictures, but try to show the progression from research through sketching, through rough model or fabric swatches, through final design and photographs of finished work," he says.

Beudert echoes this sentiment and adds that it's just like having to show your work in an algebra class. "The resulting beautiful image that demonstrates their work can be achieved in a lot of different ways. The artistic impulse that got them there is critical," he says. "You should include casual sketches and a finished product, as well as notes taken during the process that reflect how you got where you're going, particularly as we see more and more digital portfolios. The steps you took which reflect your thinking as well as your way of working are as revealing as anything else."

Teague also likes to see how potential lighting design majors achieve their finished rig. "It doesn't matter to me if you tear up a Rosco swatch book and tape it so it becomes a backlit slide, but I do like to see the colors represented graphically," he says. "I also like to see cheat sheets and hookups. A lot of that gets lost today. I really like to see realized work, obviously. Good photographs of the finished product are pretty important."

Teague feels it is advisable to keep the narrative to a minimum. "I don't know that a long, windy statement of purpose is necessarily important, but a paragraph or two about their approach to the show would be okay," Teague says. "It's important to know what impact your colleagues' work had on your lighting. What other designers did and

(Continued)

how you responded to them is not a bad thing to include, but not for every piece in the portfolio."

Beudert says that it helps him understand how the student's design process works if there is an accompanying statement of purpose with certain projects. "If they put into words what they thought about the design or work process, that indicates a process of synthesis that is important for someone going to graduate school," he explains. "Graduate school is, after all, an academic environment, and success in graduate school requires that kind of [writing] ability. If you choose to go to grad school, you can't forget about the academic aspect."

By the Book, CD, or Website

It probably goes without saying that the contents of your portfolio matter a lot more than the context, but your presentation should be somewhat aesthetically pleasing without being "slick." "It's nice to be neat and well organized," Isackes says. "Some of the most exciting students I've seen are not particularly neat or well organized, but I do look at neatness and tidiness because that's not an unimportant value."

Although Cornish does not offer an MFA, Tosti-Lane and his colleagues are heavily involved in coaching their students in proper portfolio preparation for graduate school. "We generally suggest that they arrange their portfolio with realized productions first and paper projects after, though exceptions are made when classroom work is particularly stunning," he says.

The first step that Tosti-Lane and his colleagues take in portfolio prep is having students buy the pages first rather than purchasing an expensive carrying case. The students use the pages to experiment with the best way to present their work. The next step is all about layout and deciding what goes first, second, etc., and labeling everything properly. Finally, during their last semester, students have their last public portfolio review where they present their portfolios to the entire department (faculty and students). "We also invite guests including production managers and artistic directors from local companies, other designers, and various other potential employers," Tosti-Lane says. "Students often wind up getting work from these presentations, and their portfolios are generally excellent."

Then there is the issue of whether you should have a portfolio at all, at least in traditional terms. Many students are putting their portfolios on CD, DVD, or websites. Teague is a big fan of multi-media portfolios, if, for nothing else, sheer convenience. "I think you'd be crazy not to use a website or a CD," he says. "I can see everything I need to see from a CD and it's just so convenient." He added that hand drawn work can be easily scanned and computer work can just be saved.

Tosti-Lane is very comfortable reviewing work on a website or CD—he recently received a DVD from a B.F.A. candidate—but he says that designers should not rely on just a multi-media portfolio. "If they have a really good presentation on CD or a website, then they can probably make the decision to go smaller with their paper portfolio, but there are still enough potential employers and grad school evaluators out there who are computer challenged," he explains. "If anything, I might lean toward either website or DVD at this point—DVDs are easy to make and more and more people have DVD players at home." He added that he would advise a student using a DVD portfolio to also do a simple QuickTime and Windows Media version and carry them on a CD, in case the reviewer doesn't have a computer with a DVD drive.

DVDs, CDs, and to some extent web portfolios can work especially well for a sound designer because they have the capacity to introduce time-based events. "The danger is always that you'll wind up presenting to someone who just doesn't have the gear to play back your presentation," Tosti-Lane says. "I suppose the fallback is to always bring something that you can play it on—laptop, portable player, etc. But do not commit yourself solely to this technology; always have a real, honest to goodness, hold-it-in-your-hand-and-turn-the-pages portfolio."

A digital portfolio does, however, give a professor an instant insight into a student's ability, and Beudert likes being able to get that first impression of a student's work. "However, I always need to see the real thing at some point because I think there's an awful lot a digital portfolio can mask," he says. "It's easier to oversell your work in a digital portfolio. I would certainly take in a student after having only seen their work in a traditional portfolio but I can't say the same is true with only a digital portfolio." He added that sound designers in particular can benefit from a mostly digital portfolio but that he needs to see how visual artists draw, paint, and draft, even if it is only in CAD.

"I think it is quite telling how students present their work," Beudert continues, "although some students may not be terribly well coached. However, when you speak with a student you try to establish a connection to their work. I prefer to encounter a student who has an artistic investment in their work but their skills may need improvement and that's what graduate school can do. The reason you're going to school is that you want to learn more. If you were perfect, there'd be no need to go to grad school, and that's less of an interest to me."

Beudert added that he has seen portfolios that are, in a word, fantastic, and he encourages those students to skip graduate school altogether. "Quite frankly, what are they going to get out of three years in school when they probably need to spend that time working in theatre, whereas other students need that environment and could benefit from grad school [in order to improve their design skills]. What graduate school can't do is create a passion that isn't there."

Everybody Says Don't!

Even MFA design faculty have their pet peeves. Here are a few missteps to avoid when assembling your work for review:
- Leave out your professors' projects, no matter how much you helped.
- No basic scene painting projects. Everyone has those.
- Leave out bad, sloppy, or illegible work or drawings (duh).

(Continued)

- Don't put in too many photos of the same type of show. Demonstrate variety.
- A neat portfolio will not disguise a lack of ability. But don't be haphazard or sloppy either.
- No reviews, certificates, or letters of recommendation, but do keep these things handy (in a pocket or a folder).
- Only include projects you truly believe in.
- Make sure each project is clearly labeled.
- Do not include any bowls of candy or other snacks at a portfolio review; it won't make anyone like your work more.

No Techie Left Behind . . .

Just because you are pursuing an MFA as a stage manager, technical director, or sound designer does not mean you should relegate your portfolio to a simple resume and transcript. You should also be well versed in the various technical languages as well as a commitment to collaboration. But, just like everyone else, you need to show your work, processes, and finished product.

Sound Designers: Sound designers should be able to sketch out a visual representation of their speaker location in a set, so be sure to include speaker diagrams, equipment lists, checklists, cue lists, etc. Be able to communicate your ideas as an artist, not just your equipment choices and the physical layout of the system. "Your research probably needs to be even more thorough than the other designers, because many people will not be used to thinking of sound other than in terms of specific cues, volume, and so on," says Tosti-Lane. It is also recommended to include a CD of carefully prepared examples, along with a method for playback (laptop, CD player with headset, etc.).

Technical Directors: TDs need to show that they are more than the just person who builds the sets. Show that you are a master of many skills but especially adept with collaboration, organization, and graphic presentation. "A good TD can make everyone else's work so much easier, but a lackluster TD can make everyone's life difficult," Tosti-Lane says. Realized projects are really key for a TD's portfolio, as well as carefully documented examples of how the process was moved forward by your proactive efforts.

Stage Managers: Demonstrate your organizational drive; communicate just how comfortable the director, design team, and actors will be under your hand. You should show an understanding of all the various skills, but you need not show proficiency in each one. However, you should include your drawings and your work in at least one design area. Also, be sure to have at least one complete prompt book and examples of the forms you used to give an idea of your methodology. "They need to convince the reviewer that they can communicate with everyone on the team, and that they know how to deal with the difficult people as well as the pussycats," Tosti-Lane says.

■ THE BASICS

In the professional field, a winning portfolio would contain a combination of traditional visual representation and contemporary technology. The goal is to demonstrate the individual's capability to communicate ideas visually. Some projects can be presented in traditional ways through renderings, perspectives, and production photographs; other projects may have to be contextualized with period research, process photographs, and digital technology.

Professionals interviewing for a job should assume that directors and pro-ducers will look for the talents and expertise that best match a designer or technician to a specific project. They may be interested in the individual's capability to abstract and use metaphor for a conceptual piece or they may be looking for someone who is excellent at research and style sheets for a historical piece. It is important that the applicant's work demonstrates a variety of skills and processes.

Design–tech portfolios should show a good understanding of perspective, drafting, and two-dimensional and three-dimensional work, in addition to having clear and impressive layouts. Each discipline may rely on specific formats due to the nature of the work, but some projects may require non-traditional approaches. For example, a lighting project for a dance-theatre piece may require color renderings to clearly show the director the lighting design style for the piece. Another instance would be a costume design for a special-effect creature; this may require drafting or sections to explain how the actor wears and handles the mechanics of the garment.

■ THE SPECIFICS: SCENIC, COSTUMES, LIGHTING, AND SOUND

| SCENIC

Projects in a scenic design portfolio would include concept and inspirational art sources; research and style sheets; specialty materials sources; draftings, such as ground plans and sections (traditional and digital); innovative ideas and solutions; perspectives and elevations (traditional and digital); swatches and material samples; photographs of models and processes; and photo-graphs of final sets and performances for fully realized projects.

Brian Prather earned his M.F.A. at Brandeis University. His scenic work includes the premiere production of "Fuente" for the Barrington Stage Company, the premiere of "My Heart and My Flesh" for Coyote Theater at Boston Playwright's Theater, "First Love" for StageWorks Hudson, and "Thief River" for the Barrington Stage Company. I enjoyed working with him and had an opportunity to observe his work (first-hand) for the production of the musical "Working" for Emerson Stage at the Cutler Majestic Theatre in 2004 (Figure 4.1). His portfolio pages for this project help illustrate some of the comments discussed in Mark Newman's article.

Figure 4.1
(a) Brian Prather's scenic portfolio page. It includes (from top to bottom) a photograph of the realized production of "Working," various sketches and perspectives of different scenes, and some research photographs used for inspiration.

Figure 4.1 (cont.)
(b) Brian Prather's sketch detail (notice the quality of his hand drawing).

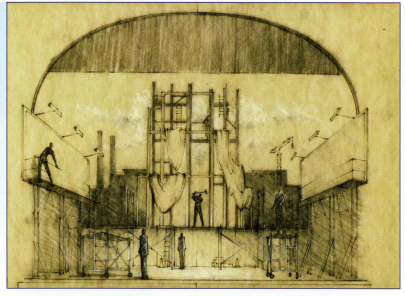

Figure 4.2
(a) Concept and
research plates
for the opera
"Rigoletto."

COSTUMES

Projects in a costume design portfolio would include concept, research, and cut sheets; preliminary sketches (if process is key to the project); color palettes; finished sketches; construction notes; garment detail draftings; and fabric and trim swatches. If a project involves crafts, then fabric paint and distress samples would be necessary. Amanda Monteiro, a former student at Emerson College, did successful layouts for nonproduced (class) projects, paying close attention to the graphics chosen for display. For the opera "Rigoletto" (Figures 4.2a–c), she included her research plates and watercolors.

The costume design portfolio would also include photographs of finished garments and performances for realized projects. Donna Meester, who is head of the MFA & undergraduate Costume Design and Production Program at the University of Alabama, suggests that, for large shows, particularly those with identifiable groups, one way to organize the presentation is by groupings of such groups (Figure 4.2d). When these pages are included in a portfolio, they can be presented with the research and photograph pages, with the painted sketches being located next to the group to which they belong (Figure 4.2e). Another presentation would be to have all of the research and photograph pages together followed by the complete set of sketches. Do not feel compelled to include one sketch per page. If more than one fits, use the space.

LIGHTING

In the article at the start of this chapter, Mark Newman states that "Drawing is also imperative from a lighting design point of view, especially examples

Figure 4.2 (cont.)
(b) Watercolor sketch for "Rigoletto" (of the main character).

Figure 4.2 (cont.)
(c) Famous quartet scene from "Rigoletto."

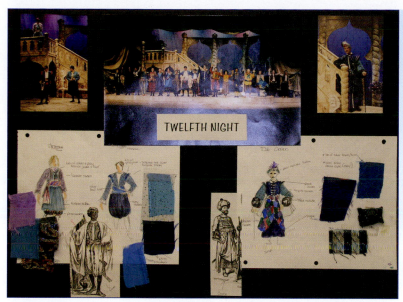

Figure 4.2 (cont.)
(d) Donna Meester's portfolio page for "Twelfth Night" (produced at the University of Louisiana–Monroe); the page layout includes a group sketch with notes and fabric swatches.

of hand drafting, which should not be ignored just because computer drafting is available". A lighting designer must be able to demonstrate the ability of hand-draft. Computer renderings can be featured in the profolio layout; but the originals must be available either folded between pages or in the protfolio's back pocket.

Projects in a lighting design portfolio would include light plots and sections, cue sheets, samples of special effects, technical paperwork (as needed), and photographs of final designs and performances of fully realized projects. Occasionally, and depending on the project, it could also include inspirational research photographs, drawings or watercolor washes on a set elevation, as well as color gel swatches. Anthony Phelps (featured in Chapter 1) is the Associate Technical Director at Harvard University. His portfolio pages illustrate some of the points mentioned above (see Figures 4.3).

Figure 4.2 (cont.)
(e) Donna Meester's portfolio page for "Twelfth Night" (produced at the University of Louisiana–Monroe); the page layout includes sketches, research, and production photographs.

Figure 4.3
(a) Anthony Phelps' light plot sample; the photograph shows a small sample of a light plot on a portfolio plate for "Romeo and Juliet."

Figure 4.3 (cont.)
(b) Anthony Phelps' magic sheet sample; the photograph shows a small lighting magic sheet on a portfolio plate for "Romeo and Juliet."

Figure 4.3 (cont.)
(c) Anthony Phelps' photograph sample; detail shot of the set and lights for "Romeo and Juliet" showing the detail of the balcony.

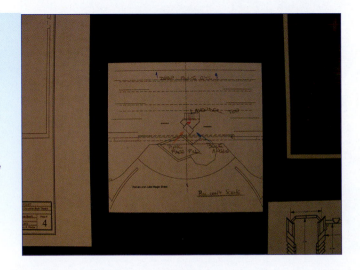

|SOUND

Projects in a sound design portfolio would include design concept narrative (as needed), sources research, cue sheets, microphone pack plots, and CD samples. Sometimes it is helpful to show photographs of key moments from a fully realized production with sound cues added to them. Andy Leviss, a freelance sound designer, says: "A good example of a divider page for a show should include a number of production shots—a good way to add visuals to a portfolio for a nonvisual design medium (Figure 4.4a),—a couple

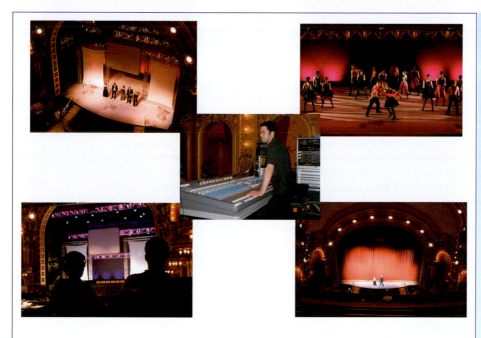

The 22nd Annual EVVY Awards
May 17, 2003
Cutler Majestic Theatre
Boston, MA

Producer: The EVVY Awards
Director: Leah Farrell

The EVVY Awards are a live telecast awards show, styled after the Emmy and Oscar broadcasts, produced annually by students at Emerson College in Boston, MA. After working as an audio assistant and then associate sound designer and front-of-house engineer for the 19th and 20th shows respectively, I was asked to design both the front-of-house and broadcast sound systems, as well as all music and effects playback for both the 21st and 22nd shows. The design included coordinating complex playback systems from the broadcast truck with upwards of 40 live sources onstage and various other sources dedicated to the broadcast/webcast feed, while overseeing a crew of three additional engineers and four technicians.

Documents Included:
Rental Package Bid Specifications
System Block Diagrams
System Patch Sheets

Figure 4.4
(a) Divider page for one of the shows featured in sound designer Andy Leviss' portfolio.

of 'eye candy' shots of the FOH sound system, a brief description of the show and what its design entailed, and a listing of what documentation from the show is included in its section of the portfolio."

Leviss continues: "A project should include a sample page from the bid specifications that were sent out to potential bidders for the show's rental package (Figure 4.4b)—useful for producers to view your ability to commu-

---

Figure 4.4 (cont.)

(b) Sample of sound designer Andy Leviss' bid specifications that were sent out to potential bidders.

The 22nd Annual **EVVY** *Awards*, Audio Bid Specs.   2/3

Mixing Consoles
1 - Analog console with minimum of 32 input channels, 8 group busses, L/R/M output busses, 6 matrix outputs, 8 mute groups, and mute scene automation (Midas Heritage preferred, other brands/models that meet all spec's may be acceptable upon consultation with designer, Mackie or Behringer consoles are **not** acceptable under any circumstances).
1 - Shure SCM410 four channel automatic mixer

Microphones
4 - Shure MX418/C 18" Gooseneck Microphone w/shock mount
10 - Shure ULX1 wireless microphone transmitters with Sennheiser MKE-2, DPA 4060, Shure WL50, Countryman B3, or Countryman B6 lavalier element
2 - Shure ULX2 wireless microphone transmitters with Shure Beta 87c element
12 - Shure ULXP4 frequency-agile dual-diversity wireless microphone receivers
4 - Dual microphone alligator/tie-bar clips for above-listed lavalier elements
2 - Powered UHF antennae (with appropriate distribution amplifier for above-listed receivers and min. 25* coaxial cable for each antenna)
5 - Crown MB-4 boundary microphones w/cable
4 - AKG C568B 10" shotgun microphones
2 - Shure VP88 Stereo Microphone (w/swivel adapter and appropriate 5-pin XLR-F to 2 3-pin XLR-M Y-cable)
2 - Shure KSM44 microphone (w/shock mount) (Electro Voice RE20 is also acceptable)

Processing
1 - DOD SR400D Digital Room Delay (2 channels in/out)
4 - BSS DPR-404 Quad Compressor/De-esser
1 - Aphex Compeller
4 - stereo 1/3 octave, 31 band Klark-Teknik equalizers (Other brands may be acceptable upon consultation with desinger, Rane or Behringer units are **not** acceptable under any circumstances) (total 8 channels)
4 - Yamaha SPX 990 digital effects processors

Playback Equipment
2 - Sony CD players with balanced XLR outputs and auto-cuing of next track at end of current track

Splitters
1 - 56 channel isolated splitter (XLR inputs, Whirlwind mass connector outputs, ground lift on each channel)

Cables
10 - Appropriate insert cable pairs for above-listed analog console (min. 5' length)
8 - 5' TRS 1/4" patch cables
2 - 150' 56-pair multi-cable with Whirlwind MASS connectors on both ends
2 - 50' 56-pair multi-cable with Whirlwind MASS connectors on both ends

06/06/2005, 12:34 AM

nicate the gear you need in a clear fashion, regardless of whether they're interviewing you for a show that will be bid or just one that will be stocked from an in-house shop."

Leviss also includes block diagrams of the sound system for each show (Figure 4.4c): "One or two, in this case (although many shows will have lots more). This is the most visual that a sound design portfolio often gets. It has the benefits of both being very obvious in what it is, even to a non-technical producer, as well as generally just looking impressive".

Figure 4.4d shows "part of the patch sheets used to actually set up and cable the show when loading it in the theater," Leviss says. "They actually contain much of the same information as the block diagram, but in a format that's easier to reference for the purposes of setting up the console and running cables; the idea here is to show that in addition to actually designing the system, you can translate the information into a way that's easy for the crew working for you to set it up quickly and without confusion."

TECHNICAL DIRECTORS, COSTUME TECHNICIANS, AND MASTER ELECTRICIANS

Technical directors, costume technicians, and master electricians need to show that they are more than just a person who builds or rigs the final product. In the professional world, a good technician can facilitate production and make everyone else's work so much easier. On the other hand, a lackluster technician can add challenges to the process and make everyone's life difficult. Realized projects, with their technical drawings and such, are a must in a technician's portfolio. A technician's portfolio should also include carefully documented examples of how the process was moved forward by the technician's proactive efforts.

Technical portfolios can include management-related paperwork, such as work orders, inventories, plots, cue sheets, etc. They can also include technical drawings by the technician (traditional and digital) to demonstrate the technician's understanding of and ability to solve particular design challenges, as well as photographs of the final product for fully realized projects. This type of portfolio could also include reductions of the designer's original drawings next to the technician's final product to illustrate their capability to translate design from paper to the stage. A glossary of vendor sources and network relations may also be included to indicate to designers and producers the technician's ability to facilitate access to materials and process.

As I mentioned earlier in this chapter, my colleague Anthony Phelps is the Associate Technical Director at Harvard University. He is also the founder and executive editor of *The Painter's Journal*. Anthony's portfolio includes a variety of technical drawings, sketches, and production photographs that illustrate his talent and capabilities (Figure 4.5).

For a graduating student pursuing a new job or entry into a graduate school, the format of the portfolio is as key as its content; the portfolio has to show skill, technology, knowledge, and superb organization. Andrew

Figure 4.4 (cont.)
(c) Sample of sound designer Andy Leviss' block diagrams for the sound system for a show.

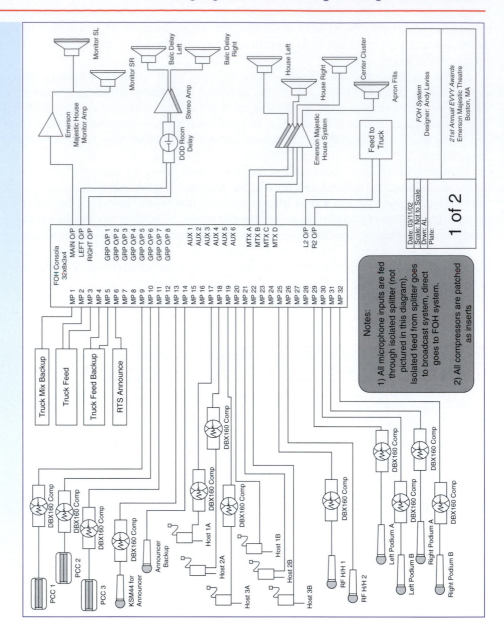

FOH Patch for 22nd Annual EVVY Awards
Andy Leviss, Sound Designer/FOH Engineer

Input Patch

Ch	Description	Snake Ch.	Splitter Ch.	Notes
1	Kick	C1	-	
2	Snare	C2	-	
3	Overhead Left	C3	-	
4	Overhead Right	C4	-	
5	Bass	C5	-	
6	Rhythm Guitar	C6	-	
7	Lead Guitar	C7	-	
8	Harmonica	C8	-	
9	Keys	C9	-	
10	Vox 1	Y-E6	22	Y'd from H/H A (18)
11	Vox 2	Y-E7	23	Y'd from H/H B (19)
12	Vox 3 (Drummer)	C10	-	
13	Ben/Shira Backup	E1	41	
14	Vanessa/Dave Backup	E2	42	
15	Seth/Chachi Backup	E3	43	
16	Evie Backup	E4	44	
17	Sarah Backup	E5	45	
18	Handheld A (Red)	Y-E6	22	Y'd to 10
19	Handheld B (Yellow)	Y-E7	23	Y'd to 11
20	Ben/Shira	E8	24	
21	Vanessa/Dave	E9	25	
22	Seth/Chachi	E10	26	
23	Evie	E11	27	
24	Sarah	E12	28	
St1	FX A Return			
St2	FX B Return			
25	Piano Bass	E13	15	
26	Piano Treble	E14	16	
27	Podium Automixer			
28	PCC 1	E15	6	
29	PCC 2	E16	7	
30	PCC 3	E17	8	
31	PCC 4	E18	9	
32	PCC 5	E19	10	
33				
34	Announcer	E20	17	
35	Announcer Backup	E21	18	
36	Playback Feed	E22	50	
37	Podium Left - Tall	E23	30	Direct Out to Automixer
38	Podium Left - Short	E24	29	Direct Out to Automixer
39	Podium Right - Tall	E25	32	Direct Out to Automixer
40	Podium Right - Short	E26	31	Direct Out to Automixer

Figure 4.4 (cont.)
(d) Sound designer Andy Leviss' patch sheets used to actually set up and cable the show when loading it in the theatre.

Figure 4.5
(a) Anthony Phelps' paperwork presentation; he uses black matboards for his display instead of portfolio sheet holders. The paperwork includes draftings, technical drawings, spec sheets, and shopping lists.

**Figure 4.5
(cont.)**
(b) Anthony
Phelps'
presentation
pages; each
storyboard
includes
research,
sketches, and
production
photographs.

Kirsch was a student I had the opportunity to coach. His is a very good example of a well-balanced technical director portfolio; it shows that as a technician he is able to solve problems and make fantastic things happen (Figure 4.6).

**Figure 4.5
(cont.)**
(c) Samples of
Anthony Phelps'
work.

Figure 4.6
(a) Andrew Kirsch's opening page; notice how he includes digital information and a résumé at the start.

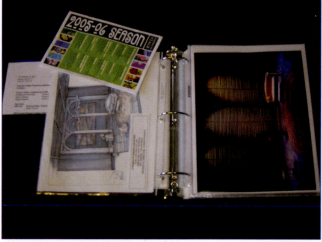

Figure 4.6 (cont.)
(b) Andrew Kirsch's first project is one of his strongest; he starts with a bang! These pages feature sketches, draftings, CAD drawings, shopping lists, technical details, processes, and final pictures for the production of "Undiscovered Country," produced by Emerson Stage in 2005 (director, Kent Stevens; set design, Timothy Jozwick; costume design, Angela Markman; lighting, Kristin Hayes).

Figure 4.6 (cont.)
(c–e) Pages from Andrew Kirsch's portfolio; notice the use of foldout pages and inclusion of technical solutions. He was in charge of solving and rigging three large blinds that covered three large arches during different scenes.

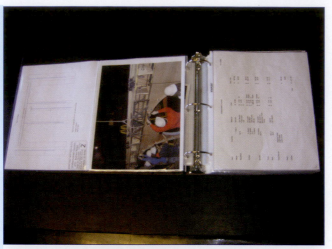

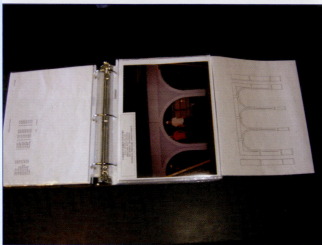

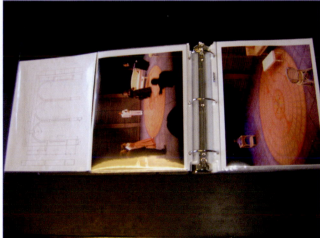

Figure 4.6 (cont.)
(f–g) Andrew Kirsch also had the challenge of figuring out the technical scale labyrinth path depicted in the original rendering of the floor plan. These pages show how the original set design translated to a CAD plan, the floor in process, and the finished product.

Now that we have reviewed some specifics about what to include in a portfolio, what are some of the things to avoid and what new technologies do we need to be aware of?

WORKBOOK: CHOOSING SPECIFIC BODY OF WORK   WHAT IS MY PORTFOLIO CONCENTRATION? WHAT WORK DO I NEED TO INCLUDE IN MY PORTFOLIO? WHAT WORKS DO I NEED TO COLLECT IN ORDER TO PLAN MY LAYOUTS?

Chapter 5

Portfolio Development Techniques: Do's and Don'ts

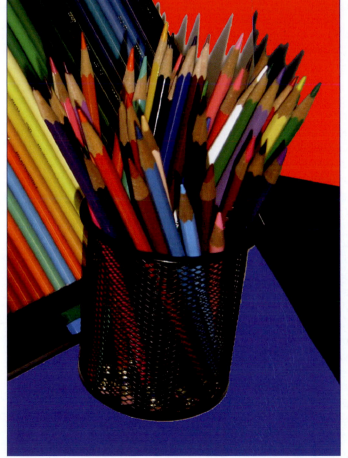

Experienced professionals and seasoned academicians would most likely agree that there are common guidelines to consider when developing a portfolio. While there are no hard-set rules, some standards do apply. This section will look at some commonly accepted practices and practices to avoid. I will call these the *do's* and the *don'ts* of portfolio development.

PORTFOLIO DEVELOPMENT DO'S: GOOD PRACTICES

In previous chapters, we established that the process of developing a design–tech portfolio is not all that different from the process that takes an idea from a two-dimensional drawing to a final product on the stage. It takes clear vision and hard work. In order to create an effective showcase, designers and technicians need to set goals, edit and organize materials, choose layout supplies, and provide information about their projects in a way that best features their work.

Most reviewers will say that a portfolio must be put together in such a way that it answers questions specific to its goals. A portfolio prepared for graduate school will have to meet different expectations compared to one used to apply for jobs as a designer or technician in regional theatre. Donna Meester, Assistant Professor in the Department of Theatre and Dance at the University of Alabama, has reviewed many portfolios while serving as the Design Chair for the Kennedy Center American College Theatre Festival. She recommends making the individual's goals the focus of the portfolio. "You may be a fantastic technician," she says, "[but] if you are looking for more design opportunities focus on the design work that you have done. You can include your technical experience later. Whatever you focus on is what the interviewer will see as what you are most interested in." There are some pointers for students, as well, when they do not have produced shows to present. Donna recommends: "Begin the portfolio with the strongest class projects. . . . Don't forget art classes. Photography classes produce work that shows a good eye, as well. If the portfolio is full with produced work and design/technology class projects, don't be afraid to have art projects at the end of the portfolio or in a separate binder."

The project sequences, support materials, and general organization of the book are also important. They will assist in conveying the individual's capabilities. "Do start with your strongest produced work. Do only show work that you feel confident about," suggests Kitty Leech, who is on the faculty at New York University's Tisch School of the Arts Drama Department. Kitty has reviewed hundreds of portfolios while chairing the Costume Design Exam Committee for the United Scenic Artists Local 829 (a committee she has served on since 1987) and also chairing the Young Master's Award Committee for the Theatre Development Fund's Irene Sharaff Awards. Kitty states that it is important to "be able to talk about the work from a number of different points of view: concepts, process, budget. . . . Do try to include a piece of promotional material (a program or flyer not reviews), as well as a minimum of one or two sketches and production photographs for each production being shown. Do show class projects, but at the end, not at the beginning of your presentation." Donna Meester adds: "Organization, organization, organization! 'Nuff said. Detail, detail, detail! More to say here. Good design relies on attention to detail. A portfolio is no different. Starting with the sketch, lettering should be neat, edges should not be ragged, pastels need to be fixed, etc. Sketches, swatches, research, etc., should be affixed to the page neatly when put in the portfolio. While many like to present their portfolio in chronological order, the reverse may be more effective. There is no rule saying that a portfolio needs to be in any type of chronological order. I like to see the strongest (and produced) work first and then move on to weaker projects. It is nice to end with a bang!"

Final touches are important, so featured artwork should be clearly labeled, fixed, and organized. Draftings, blueprints, and CAD drawings must be a readable size. Photographs (digital and otherwise) need to be true to stage color and contain detail. Research and reference materials should include their sources and titles. News and other media articles should include dates and title pages. The goal is to give the reviewer as many contexts as possible so they can quickly understand the scale and venue of the work being presented. "Employers will equate your attention to detail in all of your work with the level of detail you put into your portfolio, so pay attention to detail. That means use a ruler, don't eyeball. Layout and design of the portfolio pages are as important as the work on the page. Keep the principles of design in mind when planning your page layout and your rendering plates. It is another opportunity to exhibit good design choices." This advice comes from Kristina Tollefson, who serves as the Vice-Commissioner for Communication for the Costume Design & Technology Commission of the United States Institute for Theatre Technology.

PORTFOLIO DEVELOPMENT DON'TS: BAD PRACTICES

If clear goals, good organization, and specific context information are key aspects to consider when developing a successful showcase, then vague goals, bad organization, and incomplete information are the bad practices to avoid. What lessens the impact of a portfolio? "Ill-organized materials, incomplete projects, and pages that must be turned a different way for each picture" is William Gordon Henshaw's answer. Henshaw is a member of USITT, and his awards include The Kennedy Center American College Theater Festival Regional Costume Design Nominee, the Bernice Prisk Award for Excellence in Theatrical Costuming, and the Wendell Johnson Award for Excellence in Design. He also considers "too much information spread over too many pages" a distraction from the goals of the portfolio. The amount of materials on display and the handling of the portfolio will influence outcome as well. Donna Meester suggests: "Do not include the kitchen sink! You may have many projects or many pages per project that you want to include . . . [but] most interviews have a limited time frame. Include only what is most effective in showing your abilities. If it is difficult for you to eliminate, ask a friend or mentor to help you clean house."

Luckily, a portfolio is an ongoing process so anyone at the receiving end of feedback can immediately act upon that feedback. April Bartlett is a graduate student working on her M.F.A. at Carnegie Mellon, with a Scenic Design concentration. She received a Meritorious Achievement in Scenic Design Award from the American College Theatre Festival in 2004. She has recommendations that could be useful to any designer and technician: "Don't apologize for anything in your portfolio. If it requires an apology it probably doesn't belong in it. If your pictures don't look good, it doesn't matter how good it looked in real life. Become your own photographer."

Now that we have gained awareness in regards to good practices and things to avoid when developing a portfolio, how do we prepare ourselves for presentation and marketing?

Part II

Introduction to Digital Portfolios

Chapter 6
The Effective Digital Portfolio

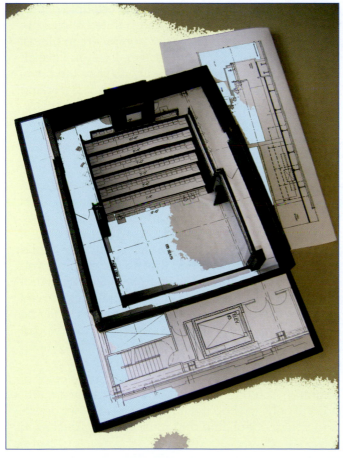

We can all agree that, in today's world, digital technology helps create new pathways that enable easy sharing of artistic ideas, research, and design. It can also facilitate communication and speed up problem solving. A digital portfolio is such a pathway, but it is important to understand that it does not replace the traditional case with original artwork. Its practicality is what makes it appealing; it is easy to copy, change, carry, and mail. Digital files make it easy to share information among designers, technicians, directors, producers, managers, school programs, and others. Even so, some may consider digital technology to be an unnecessary expense of money and time. Others may challenge its value in comparison to such basic abilities as drafting, rendering, or painting. The intent of this chapter is to explore how the design–tech process is enhanced through the use of digital files and how the traditional methods and new ones can complement each other for better results. It will also look at practical matters such as what digital portfolios are for, what information is important to keep, and how it should be stored. It is important to note that a digital portfolio will open many doors when used in combination with other traditional items such as résumés.

I turned to Carrie Robbins (one of my mentors at NYU) for information about computer use in theatrical design. She has been a Master Teacher of Costume Design at NYU for more than 25 years. She has designed costumes for more than 30 Broadway shows and many operas, films, and television programs and has received multiple Tony Award nominations. She has been a pioneer in the use of digital technology to produce sketches. Her article "Theatre Designers and Computers" (published in *Theatre Design & Technology*, Vol. 38, No. 4, 2002) raises many points to consider when using computer technology in the design–tech process.

Theatre Designers and Computers

by Carrie Robbins

We're all familiar with the arguments on both sides of the debate about using computers in the design studio. Some designers lament the mechanical look of pictures created with computers. Why, they ask, should I spend thousands of dollars on computer hardware and software and spend countless hours learning to do something that I can already do quite well using simple, inexpensive tools like paper, charcoal, pencil and watercolors? Other designers argue that drawing and painting software is very sophisticated these days and capable of producing renderings every bit as expressive as hand-painted ones. I am one of the growing number of designers who use computers in almost every aspect of their work. Of course, a hand-drawn, freehand sketch can never be duplicated by a machine, and I really do miss the physical sensation of a pencil biting into a fresh sheet of paper, but working in the digital realm gives me some capabilities that I never had before.

Working with Collaborators

All theatre design evolves. Sometimes swiftly and easily, but more often it takes many rough starts to conceive something that everyone likes: the director, the choreographer, the writer, the producers, the stars, etc. There is never enough time to draw, re-draw and rework, especially if you must start from scratch with each sketch. Or, have you ever had a new idea late in the process? And having had that new idea, have you had enough time, or even what I call psychic energy, to sketch out that new idea and risk chucking the previous, almost totally approved scheme? Have you thought to yourself, "This new idea may actually be a much better solution, but how long will it take me to get it to the point where it is presentable to a team of non-designers who (rightfully) need help visualizing an idea?" And so you don't mention it.

Or do you use your sketches to help yourself visualize the color of the gown you're designing? You paint it blue but wonder how it might look in a different shade. If only you had the time to paint another option to see for yourself. But you're out of time and must get the sketches to the shop.

Or you're working with a director who demands a bright fuchsia dress. You spend many hours making the best fuchsia dress you can. The response when you show the dress to the director—which you might have anticipated—goes like this: "Well, I know I said fuchsia, but actually I think, on reflection, and now that I see it, peach would be better." This has happened to me, and I have been quite annoyed. I paint slowly, and as I fumed all I could think about was how much more time it was going to take me to produce a sketch that I could even tolerate looking at for the length of the build. (It's my nemesis that I care too much for the sketch itself. I want everyone to see a fully realized sketch because I think it helps them, if only as an inspiration. Besides, creating a detailed sketch involves making decisions that are vital to people who will build the costume.) Now, changes are not so traumatic. Changing fuchsia to peach is literally just a few clicks away, and I remain a happy camper.

I have found that I make costume decisions more clearly if the colored ground I'm using for my costume sketches is similar to or connected somehow to the dominant color of the set. I believe it's easier for directors to make informed judgments about clothes if they can see them relative to that ground. So, when I hear that the set designer has changed the background colors of the scene, I love being able to revise my ground color with a few clicks. I also love being able to paint light over dark without having to spray-fix the dark tone, or put a thick layer of some non-bleed glop over the area I want to change, or paint the new, lighter section on a different piece of paper and meticulously cut it out with my surgical scissors so the patch doesn't show and glue it into place. Only Maxfield Parrish does this trick undetectably!

I have yet to find a look or a medium I can't mimic fairly accurately using standard computer painting software—oil, charcoal, transparent or opaque watercolor, chalk, marker, etc. I often find myself creating effects that I never would have thought of working traditionally. I love this kind of graphic surprise; the happy accident. Besides, if I want to draw on a piece of paper, I can do that whenever I want.

If you're a set designer working with a director who truly has trouble visualizing space, and you don't have time or money for assistants to make clear scale models, mightn't it be useful to sit at a computer and show such a director various layouts of furniture, walls, doors, etc., each on it's own layer so that it can move independently anywhere on the stage or disappear with a click? How cool is that?

If you're a set or costume designer needing to revamp a gaggle of sketches quickly, and you don't want to give away half of your fee hiring a sketch artist for the job—or if you're on the side of that old argument about the efficacy of having another person do that work, who believes that the person doing a major portion of the sketching is the person doing the designing—then learning enough about the computer just to make those revisions or variations might be well worth investigating. Pushing oneself up and over the computer's learning curve is really not so awful.

Relearning and Learning for the First Time

Relearning how to draw using a computer probably isn't for you if you aren't the kind of person who enjoys "going back to school." However,

(Continued)

it is true that once you learn one program, learning how to use other ones is much easier. Basic computer-drawing skills—using the mouse, using a graphics tablet and a stylus, getting used to looking at a computer monitor while you draw, etc.—are applicable to all the drawing/painting programs you will eventually use. I know that some computer artists are quite skilful drawing with a mouse but I am not. I use a Wacom graphics tablet because using the stylus (they come cordless now) is fairly similar to working with a pen or pencil. In fact, most drawing programs are able to take advantage of pressure-sensitive technology built into graphics tablets, allowing you to make thick, heavy lines, or light, thin ones depending on how hard you press with the stylus.

My students at NYU's Tisch School of the Arts, Department of Design for Stage and Film, have talents that often only emerge while learning to use computers. Some students of costume design who never considered it possible to draw the simplest of rooms in decent perspective have created amazing spaces within two weeks of learning Photoshop. Set designer students who normally shy away from drawing figures have produced wonderfully sensitive portraits in Painter. And lighting design students who often have difficulties with both figures and freehand perspective have created persuasive environments as well as impressive figures. All the students I've worked with have created sophisticated work in no more than two or three weeks of targeted study per program.

Figure 6.1
(a) Patterned room color and texture study by student designer Jennifer Paar; notice the use of inventive patterns to create a mood.

Figure 6.1 (cont.)
(b) Patterned room color and texture study by student designer Jo Winlarski. There is potential in every textural bit of this study; by testing different patterns and practicing different omputer skills (such as selection, filling, copying, etc.), a designer can sharpen these skills.

When I teach computer drawing/painting, I limit our work in each software program to only what's most important for the specifics of theatre design, which I guestimate might be as little as 15% of each program's full capability. We cover three programs—Photoshop, Painter and Illustrator—and I let the students decide which, if any, is most comfortable or useful for them in design work once they complete the course. I stress that our goal is to learn to use these new tools artistically, not just technically. I also remind them that, even though learning how to use computers requires logical and somewhat technical thinking, eventually they will feel proficient and will be able to concentrate on creating works of art.

New Capabilities and New Uses

When designing the clothes for the musical "Rags," I wanted to create fabrics that were printed with images we associate with immigrants: photos of people at Ellis Island and aboard ships, lists of names on ships' manifests, etc. Handpainting these images would have been prohibitively expensive for the production at Papermill Playhouse, but I was able to acquire authentic images, arrange them to suit the patterns of the clothes, and then have them printed on an ink-jet fabric printer.

(Continued)

Figure 6.2
(a) From "Rags," study for an immigrant woman drawn by Carrie Robbins using Painter and Photoshop.

Figure 6.2 (cont.)
(b) For "Rags," Carrie Robbins used computer-assembled graphics printed onto fabric using an ink-jet printer to achieve a handpainted effect. Period research is superimposed on several gores of a skirt.

Figure 6.2 (cont.) (c) Sample garment for "Rags" constructed from ink-jet-printed fabrics.

Image research is an essential part of designing any show. With the help of image acquiring and editing software like Photoshop, the designer can collect pictures from many (heavy) books, and other sources, and create a collage of research for use in discussions with directors and other designers. The days of dragging suitcases full of source materials to meetings, fumbling for the right pages with the yellow stickies have fallen off, are gone.

Conclusion

The beauty of the integration of computers into our work as designers is that we can show more options and make more revisions in much less time then we ever could before. While it's true that a good drawing, whether in the computer or on a piece of paper, takes the same amount of time (possibly a little longer in the computer until you get used to how to do it), the ability to make changes swiftly without your drawing looking scrubbed over is simply wonderful. It frees you to contribute many more ideas then ever before. We are seeing only the tip of the iceberg as far as artistic uses of computers. I believe that if you give a smart, talented person a new tool, he or she will figure out what to do with it. I intend to keep practicing and, hopefully, getting better. If you have discovered new ways to create your art with the help of the computer, please let me know.

Figure 6.3
(a) Research cut sheet by Carrie Robbins for "Tallulah Hallelujah," starring Tovah Feldshuh.

Figure 6.3 (cont.)
(b) Room composite by student designer Eric Hallusing using Photoshop.

WHAT IS A DIGITAL PORTFOLIO, WHAT IS IT FOR?

A digital portfolio can be considered a communication facilitator and a presentation marketing tool. With today's technology, it is not unusual to find designers, technicians, and students who are scanning their hand-drawn work and saving computers files on CD, DVD, or websites, thus creating digital portfolios that include key samples of the designers' or technicians' work. They are easy to carry, easy to copy, and easy to mail and can be posted on the web. The result is a multimedia presentation that is accessible, practical, and convenient for sharing one's work.

Many producers and directors can preview the work of a designer or technician via a website, CD, or DVD. This can lead to a personal interview requiring a multimedia portfolio that includes actual artwork or draftings so it is representative of the applicant's skill. Some specialties may benefit more than others from a digital presentation. For example, a sound designer can introduce sound and scenes in real time. We must also remember the potential employers and graduate school evaluators out there who are computer challenged; designers and technicians preparing a multimedia presentation should always plan to bring the equipment necessary to play back their digitalized work, such as a laptop or portable player.

We also have to remember that most producers, directors, and colleges still prefer to see how visual artists draft, draw, and paint. Many may also want to look at real color and texture samples. Most agree that a digital portfolio is an effective way of complementing a traditional portfolio presentation but does not replace it. Of course, this attitude could change in the future.

Given the fact that digital technology is used for portfolio presentation, what do we need to know in order to create a digital portfolio?

WORKBOOK: HOW WILL I USE A DIGITAL PORTFOLIO? WHAT SHOULD I CONSIDER BEFORE DEVELOPING A DIGITAL PORTFOLIO, AND HOW WOULD I USE IT?

Chapter 7

Digital Portfolio Production Techniques

Computers and the Internet are effective resources that allow designers and technicians to share their expertise, communicate ideas faster, and seek out new career opportunities. CDs and web pages can be used to augment traditional portfolios. In order to create an effective digital showcase, designers and technicians need to be aware of the available software, display venues, and marketing possibilities.

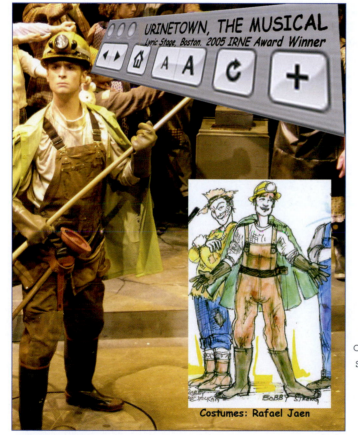

Costumes: Rafael Jaen

SOFTWARE CONSIDERATIONS

Creating a digital portfolio can be as simple as taking digital photographs of an existing portfolio and saving them on a CD. Today, Mac and PC computers have comparable programs that allow picture viewing—as thumbnails or as a slide show. It is recommended that the pictures be numbered in the order intended (for viewing) so the sequences make sense.

For more formal presentations—such as an exhibition or a lecture demonstration—programs such as PowerPoint® (Microsoft® Office™) are recommended. PowerPoint comes with various layout options; images and text can be imported into a template and can then be saved to a CD and presented as a slide show on a projection screen or monitor. People who are new to the technology need not to worry if an information technology department or a technician is not available to help; most software programs come with tutorials and web links to provide help. What is important is to take the time to experiment and practice.

Another way of sharing a digital portfolio is by maintaining a website. Files that have been saved on computers or CDs can be imported to personal websites. "While there are a number of programs that can be used to create the content of a site, Adobe Photoshop is by far my most important tool," says Kristina Tollefson, who serves as the Vice-Commissioner for Communications, Costume Design & Technology Commission of the United States Institute for Theatre Technology. Kristina finds that Photoshop is extremely easy to use and it offers many shortcuts and tricks to make repetitive tasks (such as resizing photographs or preparing image maps of graphic creation) less taxing. She adds that even renderings that are bigger than a scanner bed can be scanned a couple of times and then pieced together. "Photoshop makes piecing the images together pretty simple." Kristina is considered a wizard of digital technology among her colleagues. She earned her M.F.A. in Costume Design and Technology from Purdue University, is currently an Assistant Professor and Resident Costume and Makeup Designer at the University of Central Florida in Orlando, and is also a member of United Scenic Artists Local 829.

According to Kristina, several other graphics programs are available that can be used for specific needs: Graphic Converter™ is very good at repairing corrupted image files. Map Spinner™ is fantastic if you need to build an image map. GifBuilder can help animated GIF files, if you are interested in that. Adobe ImageReady® can help create complicated, image-heavy page layouts. After building the master image file in Photoshop, ImageReady can help divide the large image into a number of smaller images to insert into a table. It will even generate the HTML code needed to display the page online.

Kristina and her husband Jason work together on her website; they are Mac users at home but PC based at work; the programs they use are all Mac compatible. While Photoshop and ImageReady are cross-platform programs, other graphics software may not be.

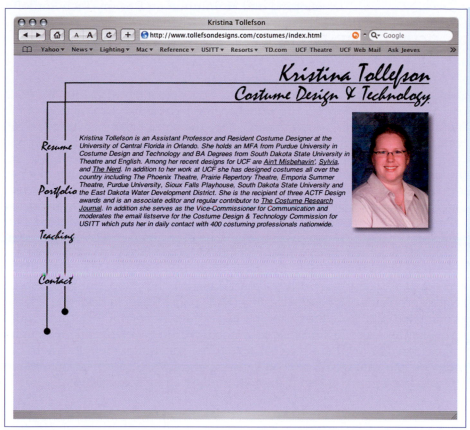

Figure 7.1

(a) Kristina Tollefson's HomePage. This is a screen capture of the homepage of her website; it serves as an introduction to those who may not know her credentials and as the main menu for the remainder of the site. The stylistic elements help set a feeling of sophistication and professionalism which are then carried through on subsequent pages.

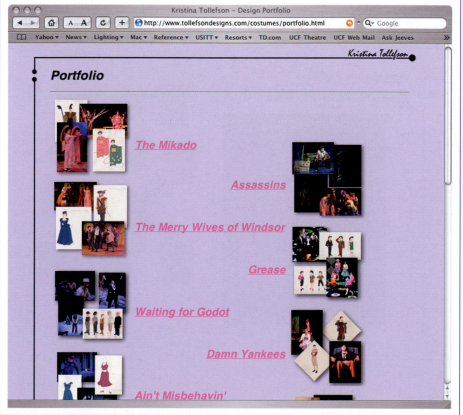

Figure 7.1 (cont.)

(b) Kristina Tollefson's Portfolio Menu: This screen capture is the main page of the portfolio section of her site. Its primary purpose is give viewers instant access to any show in the portfolio. The small collage of renderings and production shots allows viewers to better choose which shows are of interest to them. The regular arrangement of the shows is contrasted by the more organic groupings of images for each show to soften the linear nature of such lists.

■ SCALE AND DISPLAY VENUES: WEB PAGES

Sometimes taking the time to learn and experiment can pay off. "We don't use any of the WYSIWYG programs on the market like Dreamweaver® to build our web pages," says Kristina. "My husband Jason got interested in web design originally and we couldn't afford the software. So, for the price of an *HTML for Dummies* book, he taught himself the programming language instead. Many people don't realize that web pages are actually just text files containing specialized instructions which tell the web browser (Internet Explorer®, Netscape®, Safari™, etc.) what to do and how to display information. We write out all the code using a basic word processor. Our choice is TextEdit® or WordPad®, which usually come preloaded on computers. More robust word processors like Microsoft Word® can be problematic because they try to help by fixing spelling or formatting, but the HTML code doesn't follow standard written English so that help will often create bigger problems. Hand coding my web pages also makes them more streamlined and therefore faster loading. The commercial programs add a lot of extraneous code that isn't really needed and that extra code makes the pages load slower. There is a learning curve with either method. There are many people who would advocate using the software designed for creating the web pages for you and they work really well for some people."

Figure 7.2
(a) Kristina Tollefson's Assassins Show: This is the second of two pages of renderings and production shots for the musical "Assassins." The collage on the right allows viewers to select the images that appeal to them by changing the larger image on the left as they roll the cursor over the collage. The use of the collage here also brings continuity to the site structure by mimicking the smaller collage in the portfolio menu. The collage also allows the grouping of related images and characters into meaningful arrangements that give the viewer a better sense of the feel of the production.

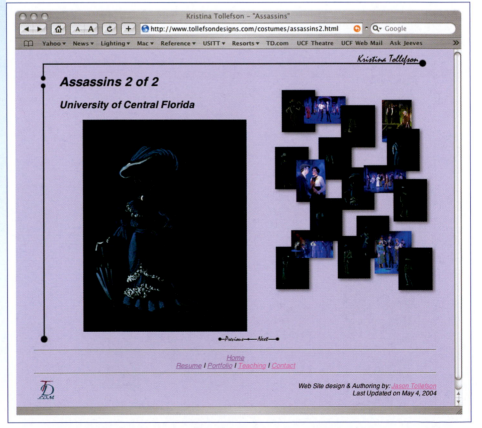

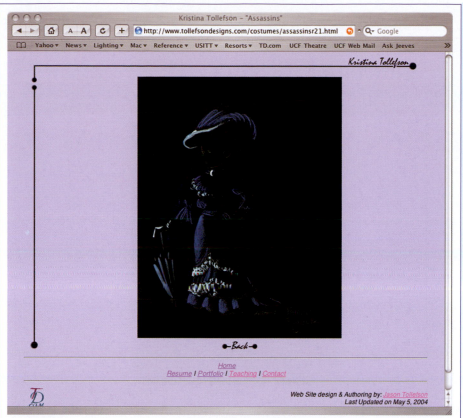

Figure 7.2 (cont.)

(b) Kristina Tollefson's Assassins Detail: The enlarged image on this page comes up when a viewer clicks on the small image in the collage menu on the previous page. I provide this enlarged image so the viewer can examine particular images in more detail if they so desire. The "Back" button takes them back to the production's collage menu.

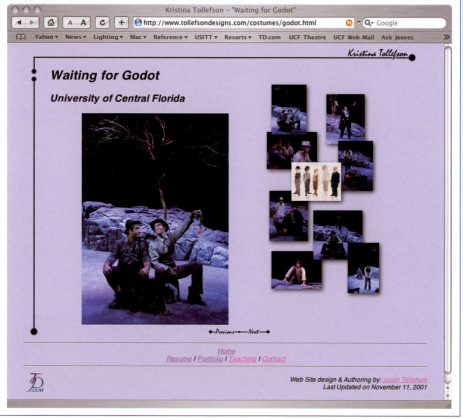

Figure 7.2 (cont.)

(c) Kristina Tollefson's Godot Show: This is another show in the portfolio. The layout on the page is exactly the same as the other productions but because of the collage menu on the right each production has an individual feel and there is no sense of monotony. The "Previous" and "Next" buttons near the bottom of the page allow the viewer to step through the entire portfolio in the order I chose if they desire or they can opt to return to the main portfolio menu page and choose any production in any order they wish.

Figure 7.2 (cont.)

(d) Kristina Tollefson's Godot Detail: This is another example of the enlarged option of each image. Notice that the basic layout of this page as well as the production overview and portfolio menu pages all have the same border surrounding the content. This helps unify the entire site and also serves as a sort of masthead for the site, branding all the content as belonging to me.

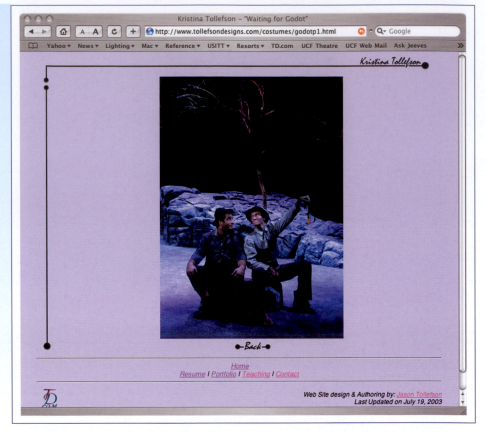

MARKETING: THE CD SHOWCASE

In order to reach as many people as possible who have different levels of computer skills, it is best to keep things simple. It is important to develop simple templates for a website. The template lets you update by plugging in content rather than starting from scratch each time. Keeping the site up-to-date is the most difficult part, and having a template makes that process much less time consuming. The layout and links must be easy to follow so the viewer can easily access the files on display and get the information needed.

Janie E. Howland is a scenic designer, a member of United Scenic Artists Local 829, an Elliot Norton Award winner, and founding member of the Cyco Scenic production company. She says: "I used to carry around a large portfolio case with images mounted onto black matboard pages. There were approximately 15 pages. Now I have an electronic portfolio. Now I carry my laptop computer and show producers a slide show of about 30 images of my work and I leave them with a disc that includes my résumé, the images, and the articles that have been published about me and my work (Figure 7.3). I still present them with a printed copy of my resume."

Figure 7.3
(a) Scanned slide from "Antigone," produced at Concord Academy High School (directed by David Gammons). The Plexiglas® panels create a "sacred space" outside of the palace, which has been boarded up and protected with barbed wire during the war in which the two brothers have killed each other.

Figure 7.3 (cont.)
(b) Set design by Janie Howland for "Sunday in the Park with George," produced by the Lyric Stage Company of Boston.

Figure 7.3 (cont.)
(c) Set design by Janie Howland for "Sunday in the Park with George," produced by the Lyric Stage Company of Boston.

Figure 7.3 (cont.)
(d) Scanned slide from "Maiden's Prayer," produced by the Huntington Theatre in Studio 210 (directed by Scott Edmiston). The set was designed to represent the fragmented memory of a "perfect" childhood. It was scattered with shadowboxes inspired by Joseph Cornell. The boxes contained frozen objects of childhood, the family estate, the perfect green grass of the backyard.

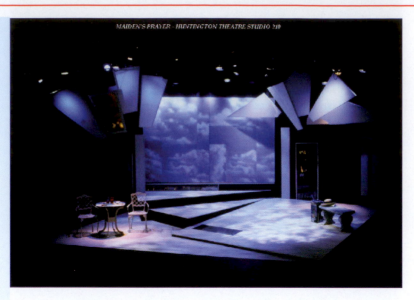

THE SLIDE SHOW: POWERPOINT PRESENTATIONS

Sometimes a digital portfolio can be used to make a presentation or to teach a class. In such cases, it is useful to turn to Microsoft's PowerPoint®. The program comes with many creative features and can be used to create presentation slides.

Figure 7.3 (cont.)
(e) Scanned slide from "Sweeney Todd," produced by the Seacoast Repertory Theatre, and directed by Spiro Veloudos. The image shows a unit set in a thrust theatre with 4 feet upstage of the proscenium walls. The set combines the many locations required by the script, including the barbershop chair that dumps customers through a trap door in the floor, onto a slide and into the pie shop oven. The paint style was inspired by Dore etchings of London.

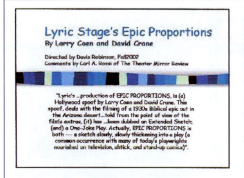
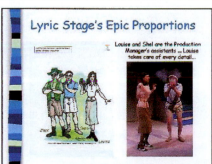

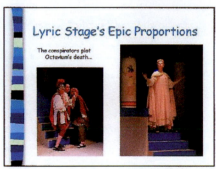
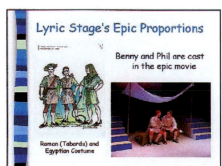
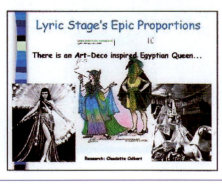

Figure 7.4
(a–b) PowerPoint slides work as a storyboard. In this sample, the concept narrative, research, costume sketches, and production photographs for the show "Epic Proportions" are conveyed by 12 slides that explain visual choices and emphasize the design elements. "Epic Proportions" was written by Larry Coen and David Crane, directed by Davis Robinson, and produced at the Lyric Stage in Boston in 2002. Costume design by the author of this book.

Figure 7.4 (cont.)
(b) PowerPoint presentations can be saved as PDF files by using Adobe Acrobat. This helps pervent viewers from altering or copying files.

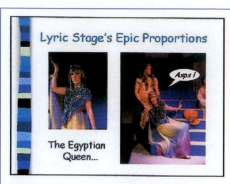

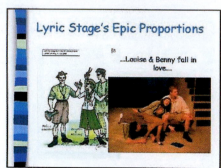

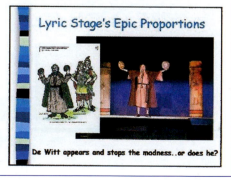

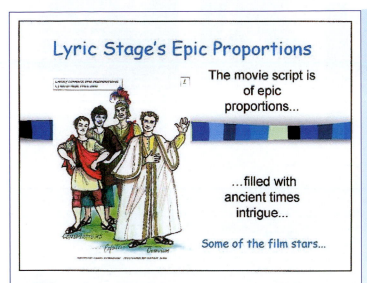

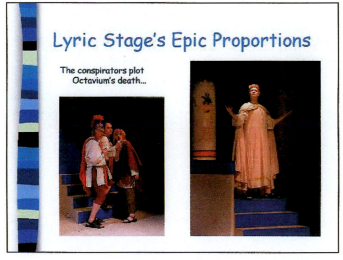

Figure 7.4 (cont.)
(c) PowerPoint features various templates and graphics that can be used to create layouts. Because "Epic Proportions" is a light comedy (the play has been dubbed an extended sketch, a one-joke play), the slide design is fun and colorful. Each frame has a sketch, comments, and production photographs. Costume design by the author of this book.

Figure 7.4 (cont.)
(d) Slide featuring costume detail for one of the main characters. This format could be used for scenic and lighting detail, as well. Costume design by the author of this book.

With PowerPoint, creating professional, unique presentations can be easy. The software offers multiple tools for keeping slides clear, well designed, and professional looking. The many layout and design options can be customized. When using PowerPoint, it is important to create slides that grab the viewer's attention by choosing the graphics carefully and treating each one of the frames as a portfolio page. Use the space on the slides effectively; include only elements that contribute to the points you want to make, and choose images that serve a purpose—such as the draftings, research, sketches, or photographs that best display your ideas. Presentations created with PowerPoint resemble a filmstrip.

THE VIRTUAL DESIGN–TECH PORTFOLIO

Ann Cudworth has worked professionally in the four realms of set design: theatre, film, television, and virtual reality. For the last 13 years, Ann has been a production designer for shows at CBS, such as "60 Minutes," "48 Hours," and special events programming. The creation of virtual scenic pieces for the 1994 election coverage started Ann's virtual set design career. Her current work can be seen on projects for "Market Watch" and CBS news promotions. She has won two Emmys, one for a real set and one for a virtual set.

Ann shared some words of wisdom when I spoke with her: "For the 'rare birds' in set design who create real as well as virtual scenery, an online portfolio works very well. A small, relatively simple, 5- to 6-page website that shows images from the designer's completed projects, as well as media clips, is easy to set up, is readily accessible to most Internet users, and will probably cost less than $200 per year to maintain. Website domain providers offer templates that allow even the most novice web designer the opportunity to produce a professional-looking website that can be viewed by anyone at all

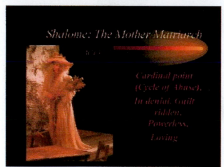
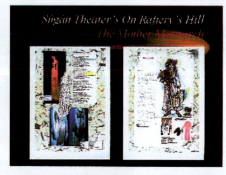

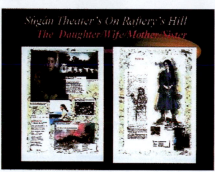

Figure 7.5
(a) For Sugan Theatre's production of "On Raftery's Hill," (written by Marina Carr, directed by Eric Engel, and presented at the Boston Center for the Arts in 2003), a darker layout and scheme were chosen. The play is a classic tragedy about family generations struggling to escape cycles of depravity visited on them. The atmosphere is rancid, and the action unmasks a truly dark world. Costume design by the author of this book.

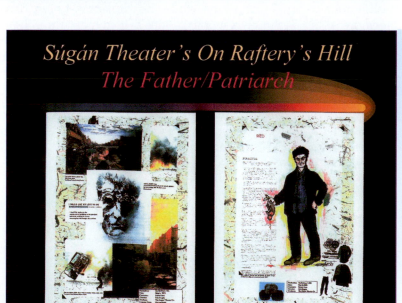

Figure 7.5 (cont.)
(b) The slide's layout matches that of a portfolio page. It includes research plates, character analyses, key dialog (that informs costume choices), and detailed sketches. Costume design by the author of this book.

Figure 7.6
Ann Cudworth says: "Website domain providers offer templates that allow even the most novice web designer the opportunity to produce a professional-looking website that can be viewed by anyone at all times." Ann Cudworth's online portfolio can be viewed at www.vsets.net.

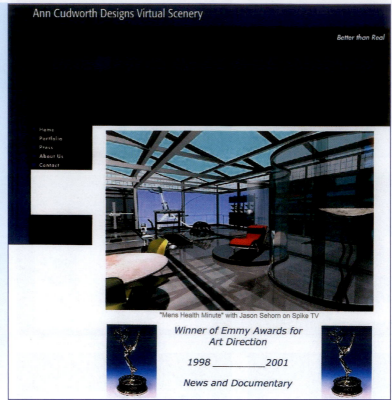

times. This is especially useful when the designer is in long distance contact with a producer and wants to discuss the portfolio during a phone chat. All the producer has to do is log on and look at the portfolio. Instant gratification! Utilizing the powerful resources of the Internet allows the designer to seek new clients, as well as provide information to existing clients, such as preliminary designs and plans while the project is being designed. Furthermore, if the designer is working with a graphics team, the images can be edited, annotated, and reworked jointly and simultaneously. All in all, for its cost vs. potential exposure, this is a very effective presentation vehicle."

Now that we have an understanding of how to prepare a traditional and a digital portfolio, we are ready for an interview. Are there guidelines for how to present our portfolio at the interview?

WORKBOOK: DIGITAL PORTFOLIO PLANNING

WHAT ARE MY GOALS? DO I WANT A WEB PAGE, A CD, OR PRESENTATION SLIDES? WHAT WORKS WILL I FEATURE AND HOW MANY PAGES WILL I DEVOTE TO EACH?

Chapter 8

Digital Portfolio Do's and Don'ts

There are some basic things to remember when planning and executing a digital portfolio to be stored on a CD or presented on a website. Always remember that the work should represent you and your skills above all.

DO'S

1. Do ask for help from your computer wizard friends.
2. Do save your work on a CD in a format compatible with both Macs and PCs.
3. Do attach a written statement with your CD explaining the contents of the portfolio.
4. Do choose the best images of completed projects, as well as media clips.
5. Do look for website domain providers that offer templates that will help you design a professional-looking site.
6. Do start your website with a few pages, keeping things simple and small.
7. Do plan for easy and inexpensive maintenance.
8. Do label things clearly and add notes as needed for instant gratification.

DON'TS

1. Don't use low-quality photographs on your website or CD.

2. Don't rely exclusively on scanning photographs; it is best to start with digital film.
3. Don't retouch pictures (e.g., color correction) to the point where they no longer look like the staged production.
4. Don't make the site all about flash and splash.
5. Don't make the website so complicated that it takes a long time to load.
6. Don't focus on the layout at the expense of the content.

Part III

Presenting and Marketing the Portfolio

Chapter 9
Portfolio Presentation Techniques

L eading experts in the field of interpersonal relations emphasize the importance of first impressions with regard to setting the communications dynamics of most relationships. During their first interviews, designers and technicians are appraised in a number of ways; it is of the utmost importance to always be prepared so productive collaborations can be forged. Good presentation skills can aid this process. In this chapter, we will review some useful techniques.

FOUNDATIONS OF PRESENTING

The online *Merriam-Webster Dictionary* defines the word "present" as an adjective, a verb, and a noun. The adjective function refers to the definition of something now existing or in progress; the verb function refers to the definition of introducing or bringing before someone; and the noun function refers to something presented, a gift or an impression. These definitions are the three keys to presenting a portfolio in a successful manner: First, the designer or technician needs to be present (now-existing, involved); second, the designer or technician needs to present (bring before) his or her work to an audience; and, third, the designer or technician needs to leave a present (lasting impression).

Being Present, Presenting and Leaving a Present

Being present refers to affect and personal appearance (Figure 9.1). Designers or technicians should be sure that they can be heard and their pronunciation is clear. They must be alert and listen to the panelists' questions carefully; voice projection and listening can create instant rapport. Another factor to consider is grooming; dressing professionally and according to the occasion will give the individual presenting a portfolio more confidence. It also signals care and commitment to future possibilities.

Presenting refers to the ability to communicate the important aspects of a project with good organization and clarity (Figure 9.2). A well-organized project should have a beginning, a middle, and an end. The layouts should show process and final product, and the pages should be properly labeled and research sources clearly acknowledged. Designers and technicians need to make sure that they have included all the necessary information, including historical period, artistic styles, source names, technical jargon, etc., so interviewers can put the information in context. Content knowledge will build trust between the parties involved.

Leaving a present refers to how the designer or technician wants to be remembered after an interview; it refers to the impression on the panelists the applicant wants to make (Figure 9.3). Are there plenty of materials illustrating the applicant's technique, artistic sense, versatility, and capabilities? Visual content, layout, and personal style can set a designer or technician apart from the rest or signal that he or she is the right one for a specific project.

Figure 9.1
Being present (illustration by former student Arika Cohen).

Figure 9.2
Presenting
(illustration by
former student
Arika Cohen).

Figure 9.3
Leaving presents
(illustration by
former student
Arika Cohen).

Figure 9.4
(a) Opening page
of the author's
portfolio.

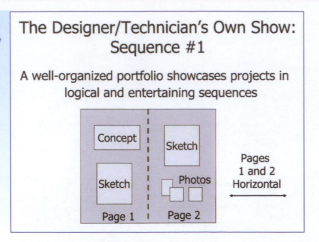

PRESENTING VISUAL CONTENT: PAGE LAYOUT OPTIONS

The visual content of a portfolio can be organized in different ways in order to best feature the work. Just like a play, each "scene" has to be integrated with the total arc of the work. Begin with an opening page for the portfolio and include a starting page for each sequence. The beginning page serves as an introduction to the designer or technician and as an introduction to the work featured in the portfolio. It must be clear and direct, as it sets the stage for the presentation. It can be as simple as an identification page or a place to hold a résumé (Figure 9.4a).

The material that follows tells the project's story. Consecutive pages need to maintain the same layout direction to guide the eye of the viewer. It is best not to display different projects next to each other to avoid confusion with regard to what the reviewer is looking at. Planning project breaks can help determine how many pages to get for a portfolio. Remember that all projects should be clearly labeled and properly keyed (Figures 9.4b–e).

**Figure 9.4
(cont.)**
(b) Horizontal
layout guidelines.

The Designer/Technician's Own Show: Sequence #2

It is helpful to maintain the same directional sequence in the layout of consecutive pages

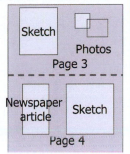

Sketch

Photos

Page 3

Pages 3 and 4 Vertical

Newspaper article

Sketch

Page 4

Figure 9.4 (cont.) (c) Horizontal layout sample from the author's portfolio.

Vertical Layout

Concept Plates, Sketches & Production Photos

Figure 9.4 (cont.) (d) Vertical layout guidelines.

Opening Title Page

Table of Contents

Figure 9.4 (cont.) (e) Vertical layout sample from the author's portfolio.

Figure 9.5
(a) Insert sample
from the author's
portfolio.

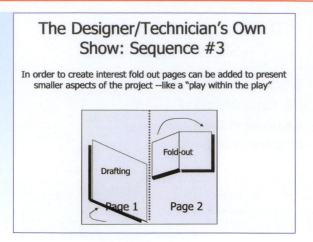

INSERTS: ADDING CONVERSATION PIECES

Other materials to consider when planning layouts include key research, process pictures, and spec information. These can be included as inserts or as loose reference materials and can serve as "conversation pieces." In order to create interest, smaller sheets can be added within a project. These smaller sheets can hold photographs, newspaper articles, research, etc. Foldout pages can be added to present smaller aspects of the project and create interest—like a "play within the play." Always make sure that the sheet holders chosen are compatible with the portfolio case to be used. The goal is to add an element of surprise, variety, and flexibility to the display (see Figure 9.5a).

To add theatricality, transitions can be created with smaller page inserts to reveal new parts of a project. Make sure that the layout helps make the portfolio pages more manageable (Figures 9.5b–d).

**Figure 9.5
(cont.)**
(b) Page inserts
and foldout
guidelines.

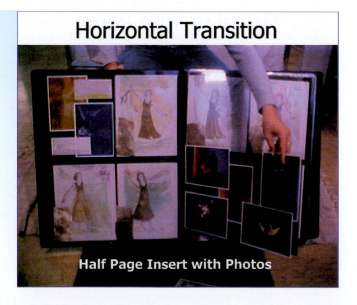

Figure 9.5 (cont.) (c) Half-page insert with photographs from the author's portfolio.

Figure 9.5 (cont.) (d) Half-page insert "reveal" from the author's portfolio.

Figure 9.6
(a) Back pocket
materials from
the author's
portfolio.

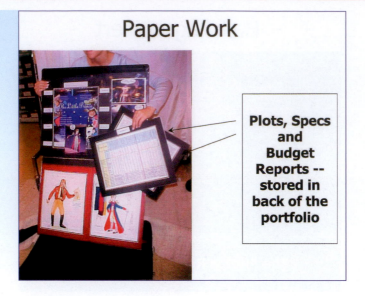

SEQUENCES: VISUAL CONTINUITY

When planning the page sequence, it is important to remember to avoid positioning horizontal and vertical pages next to each other; viewers prefer a continuous flow. Sometimes it is important to include reviews and feature articles (from major publications) to emphasize the scale and impact of the project. Support materials can be kept in a back pocket to be pulled out when describing the project. The back pocket holds extra materials that might be of interest to some of the reviewers. These are materials to be used to inform process or add clarity to a project; for example, a costume designer who has worked as a wardrobe supervisor may have costume quick-change plots to present to a production manager. Sometimes a simple three-ring binder can contain all back-pocket support materials (Figure 9.6).

**Figure 9.6
(cont.)**
(b) Page from the
author's portfolio
containing a
feature article.

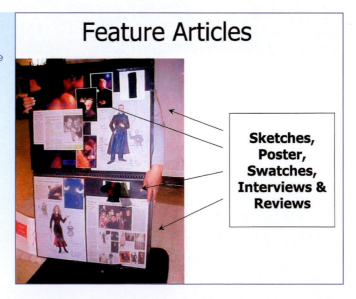

POST-INTERVIEW MAINTENANCE

Guidelines that can be helpful to both the beginner and the seasoned designer or technician in maintaining presentation skills include:

1. Remember to introduce yourself right away and take a few moments to meet the interviewers, make eye contact, share general information, etc.
2. Make sure you have plenty of current résumés and business cards to give to reviewers and prospective employers.
3. Review and update your portfolio regularly, a habit that allows you to stay in touch with your work.
4. Plan a summary for each project (basic concept, key techniques, and short anecdotes); make sure each project has a beginning, a middle, and an end.
5. Make sure the portfolio layout is clearly organized by project so it shows skill, versatility, and progress; plan transitions between projects.
6. Start strong and end strong—get the reviewers' attention and leave them wanting more.

SELF-EVALUATION

After the interview, it is important to act on any feedback in order to prepare for future opportunities. Because designers and technicians can be their own worst critics, it is important to do a self-assessment in a self-supporting, honest, and caring way. A neutral evaluation would take into consideration the panelists' feedback, future goals, and the next steps to take. A self-assessment questionnaire would include questions about style, voice, rapport, and content. These are some examples:

1. *Style*—Was my personal grooming and appearance favorable, average, or unfavorable? Why? What are the next steps?
2. *Voice*—Were my volume and articulation favorable, average, or unfavorable? Why? What are the next steps?
3. *Rapport*—Were the conversations empathetic? Did I listen well? Did I give comprehensive answers? Was this aspect favorable, average, or unfavorable? Why? What are the next steps?
4. *Content*—Were the preparation, research, work samples, and subject knowledge sufficient? Was this aspect favorable, average, or unfavorable? Why? What are the next steps?

NETWORKING: WHAT'S NEXT?

Networking refers to the creation of an ever-expanding list of future opportunities, resources, and business relations. Because most industry people refer to the design–tech field as a small community, the notion of six degrees of separation almost always applies. Designers and technicians should always keep this in mind. They should keep business affiliates' names, resources, and locations in their radar—even when they do not get the job. Such information can help with future connections and projects. At the end of a meeting, an applicant can plant the seeds for follow up (e.g., "I look forward to hearing from you soon." "I would really like to work with you." "Let's talk about possible future collaborations."). Sending a letter (before or after an interview) expressing interest in a company can open doors. Asking for feedback is also helpful; for example, if a student thinks he or she is not going to get into their first choice for a graduate program, based on the interview, that student should ask the reviewers for feedback and what course of action they would recommend. The most powerful networking tool, in my opinion, is a résumé. It can leave a lasting impression, and it can be submitted prior to an interview to create interest or left afterwards as a present.

> The résumé is one of the presents we leave after our interview—how do we make it unique? What is an effective résumé?

WORKBOOK: PREPARING THE PORTFOLIO PRESENTATION WHAT PRESENTATION TECHNIQUES DO I WANT TO FOCUS ON FOR MY NEXT PORTFOLIO REVIEW?

Chapter 10

Portfolio Presentation Do's and Don'ts

■ DO'S

1. Do plan a beginning, a middle, and an end for the portfolio presentation.

2. Do take time to meet the interviewers and establish eye contact.
3. Do project your voice and speak clearly.
4. Do remember good grooming and professional manners and appearance.
5. Do review your portfolio materials often and always prior to your interview.
6. Do plan a short summary for each project.
7. Do make sure the portfolio layout is clear.
8. Do make sure that project sequences do not compete with each other.
9. Do make sure that projects are labeled and keyed properly.
10. Do make sure to have source lists for research, materials, etc.
11. Do have support materials in the back pocket.
12. Do have updated résumés and business cards.

■ DON'TS

1. Don't present a disorganized portfolio.
2. Don't avoid looking at your interviewers.
3. Don't look like you just finished pulling an all-nighter.

4. Don't have bad grooming, including unkempt fingernails.
5. Don't forget sketch labels or keys.
6. Don't have different, competing projects adjacent to each other.
7. Don't use bad photographs or incomplete research or sketches.
8. Don't use loose pages.
9. Don't end with a weak project.
10. Don't forget to give credit to other artists' work featured with a project.
11. Don't ignore questions or get defensive.
12. Don't forget to distribute your résumé and business cards.

Chapter 11

Design–Tech Résumés, Curriculum Vitae, and Business Cards

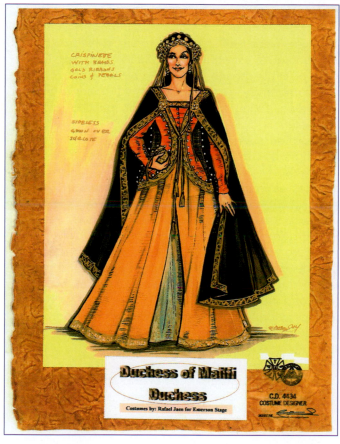

A résumé is a comprehensive document that contains a short career account of a designer or technician. It summarizes individual achievements, lists professional qualifications, and is designed with a target audience in mind. It can be one or two pages long and, when well executed, can be a most powerful networking tool. A curriculum vitae (or CV) is longer and more detailed. Whereas the goal of résumé writing is to be concise, the CV includes more details, such as education; academic background and affiliations; teaching; research experience and publications; and awards, honors, and grants. In the United States, a curriculum vitae is necessary when applying for academic, scientific, and research positions or when applying for fellowships or grants.

A Winning Résumé

In the national bestselling book, *The Pathfinderr: How to Choose or Change Your Career for a Lifetime of Satisfaction and Success* (Fireside, 1998), author Nicholas Lore describes a résumé as a "tool with one specific purpose: to win an interview." This is the number one purpose. "If it doesn't [win], it isn't an effective résumé. It presents you in the best light. It convinces the employer that you have what it takes to be successful in this new position or career." He further adds that a résumé needs to be "so pleasing to the eye that the reader is enticed to pick it up and read it. It 'whets the appetite,' stimulates interest in meeting you and learning more about you. It inspires the prospective employer to pick up the phone and ask you to come in for an interview." When planning a résumé, it is necessary to consider the goals and purpose of the document; how to list work history, experience, and education; what makes the individual special, such as awards, affiliations, and publications; and how to address personal interests, service, and references.

Intent and Purpose of a Résumé

On the Rockport Institute website (http://www.rockportinstitute.com/resumes.html), which contains excerpts from *The Pathfinder*, Lore describes the following possible reasons to have a résumé:

1. Pass the employer's screening process (requisite educational level, number years' experience, companies worked for, political affiliations, racial minority, etc.).
2. Provide contact information, such as an up-to-date address and telephone number (a telephone number that will always be answered during business hours).
3. Establish you as a professional person with high standards and excellent writing skills, based on the fact that the résumé is so well done (clear, well-organized, well-written, well-designed, of the highest professional grades of printing and paper).
4. Have something to give to potential employers, your job-hunting contacts, and professional references to provide background information and to keep in your briefcase to give to people you meet casually, as another form of a business card.
5. Use as a cover page or addendum to a job application, as part of a grant or contract proposal, as an accompaniment to graduate school or other application.
6. Put in an employer's personnel files.
7. Help you clarify your direction, qualifications, and strengths; boost your confidence; or to start the process of committing to a job or career change.

HOW TO PRESENT YOUR WORK HISTORY, EDUCATION, AND OTHER INFORMATION

"Most résumés are not much more than a collection of 'evidence' and various facts about your past," according to Lore. "By evidence, we mean all the mandatory information you must include on your résumé: work history with descriptions, dates, education, affiliations, list of software mastered, etc. All this evidence is best placed in the second half of the résumé. Put the hot stuff in the beginning and all this less exciting information afterward." He also suggests that "we divide the résumé into a 'hot' assertions section and a more staid 'evidence' section for the sake of communicating. A great résumé is all one big assertions section. In other words, every single word, even the basic facts about your history, are crafted to have the desired effect, to get them to pick up the phone and call you." The evidence includes some or all of the following.

EXPERIENCE

- List jobs in reverse chronological order. Don't go into detail on the jobs early in your career; instead, focus on the most recent and relevant jobs. (Summarize a number of the earliest jobs in one line or very short paragraph, or list only the bare facts with no position description.)
- Other headings include "Professional History" or "Professional Experience"—not "Employment" or "Work History," both of which sound more lower level.

EDUCATION

- List education in reverse chronological order, with degrees or licenses first, followed by certificates and advanced training. Set degrees apart so they are easily seen.
- Don't include any details about college except your major and distinctions or awards you won, unless you are still in college or just recently graduated.
- Include grade-point average only if it is over 3.4. List selected course work if this will help convince the reader of your qualifications for the targeted job.
- Do include advanced training, but be selective with the information, summarizing the information and including only what will be impressive for the reader.
- No degree received yet? If you are working on an uncompleted degree, include the degree and afterwards, in parentheses, provide the expected date of completion: B.S. (expected 200•).
- If you did not finish college, start with a phrase describing the field studied, then the school, and then the dates (the fact that no degree was earned may be missed).
- Other headings might be "Education and Training," "Education and Licenses," or "Legal Education/Undergraduate Education" (for attorneys).

AWARDS

- If the only awards received were in school, put these under the "Education" section.

- Mention what the award was for if you can (or just "for outstanding accomplishment" or "outstanding performance"). This section is almost a must if you have received awards.

PROFESSIONAL AFFILIATIONS

- Include only those that are current, relevant, and impressive. Include leadership roles if appropriate.

PUBLICATIONS

- Include this heading only if you have been published. Summarize them, if there are many. Include juried articles and chapter contributions to niche or specialty magazines.

PERSONAL INTERESTS

- Personal interests can indicate a skill or area or knowledge that is related to the goal, such as photography for someone in public relations or carpentry and woodworking for someone in construction management.
- This section may also be labeled "Interests and Hobbies" or just "Interests."

REFERENCES

- You may put "References available upon request" at the end of your résumé, if you wish. This is a standard close (centered at bottom in italics), but it is not necessary, as it is usually assumed.
- Do not include actual names of references. You can bring a separate sheet of references to the interview to be given to the employer upon request.

A BLUEPRINT FOR AN EFFECTIVE RÉSUMÉ PRESENTATION

When the objectives have been established and the list of credits has been sorted out, we have to plan the layout or organization of the résumé—this, of course, will depend on the number of credits to be included. Many books, software programs, and websites are dedicated to the design of the résumé and can be used as references, but the most important aspect is perhaps making sure it complements your portfolio and represents your personality and professional approach. Sometimes it is necessary to have multiple résumés (e.g., one for design and one for technical work) that can be used to apply for jobs requiring a specific talent. At times you might need to include multiple credits when the job requires multiple skills (e.g., a technical director's position that includes teaching stage craft courses and designing shows).

Remember that, just like the portfolio, the résumé will have a beginning (e.g., your name, expertise, contact info), a middle (work credits), and an end (e.g., related experience, education). For students, one page tends to be the norm; for professionals, a two-page résumé is often required. In academic settings, the curriculum vitae might be four or more pages. In all cases, the formatting must be clear and consistent, and it should be updated regularly.

When listing the work credits, it is important to include the following:

- Job title
- Type of production (e.g., show, special event)
- Date of production
- Production company, production agent, producer, etc.
- Artistic director, director, choreographer, supervisor, etc.
- Venue (e.g., theatre, television studio, museum)

The order in which these items are entered in your résumé can vary but must be consistent so the reader can make sense of the information at a glance (Figure 11.1).

Sometimes many credits have to be included, along with relevant information and notes (e.g., awards attached to a project). If more information has to be included in a résumé, then the format could be thought of as a narrative and it can be arranged in sentences or fragments, still providing the information in consistent order (Figure 11.2).

When choosing the paper and design of the résumé (e.g., fonts and type effects), make sure they represent your personality while still looking professional. Make sure the paper color and fonts will photocopy well in black and white; many a times a producer will require copies of your résumé so you should plan for it to be readable and look good when photocopied (Figure 11.3).

BUSINESS CARDS

Business cards are a personal networking tool that can highlight your personality, artistry, and area of expertise. There are many options for designing business cards; many computer programs, such as Adobe's Photoshop® or Illustrator®, include business card templates.

TIPS TO SUCCESSFUL USE OF BUSINESS CARDS AS A MARKETING TOOL OR "PRESENT"

1. The card design should be professional and attractive.
2. Cards handed out should always be in good shape and clean.

Figure 11.1
The information
in this sample
two-page résumé
includes
professional
experience,
resident design
experience,
related
experience
(teaching,
management,
community
service), and
education. This
résumé could
be used for
obtaining
freelance work as
well as work in
an academic
setting. Notice
that on page one
the name and
title at the top of
the page are
clearly legible—
contact
information is
included and
important
memberships
are highlighted.
This first page is
organized in two
columns (it could
also be organized
in three or four
columns) with
information
provided in the
same order for
each one of
the projects
mentioned. Page
two details
related
experience.

Rafael Jaen
Costume Designer
H (617) 451-1157 & W(617) 824-8359. Email: rafael_jaen@emerson.edu
Member of USA 829 Chapter 829 and USITT Costume Commission

Experience

Most Recent Works

Costume Design and Manufacturing

- **Gluck's "Alceste"**   **Producer: Opera Boston**
  Majestic Theatre, Boston, Winter 05   Director: Brad Dalton

- **T. Williams "Glass Menagerie"**   **Producer: Lyric Stage**
  Lyric Stage Theater, Boston, Winter 05   Director: Eric Engel

- **Shakespeare's "Merchant of Venice"** **Producer: Publick Theatre**
  Soldiers Field Road, Charles River   Director: Diego Arciniegas
  Boston, Summer 04

- **M. Carr's "On Raftery's Hill"**   **Producer: Sugan Theater Co.**
  Boston Center for the Arts, Sprg 03   Director: Eric Engel

- **"Triple Exposure" & "Free Fall"**   **Producer: Ipswich Moving Co.**
  Dance Complex, Cambridge &
  Boston Center for the Arts, Wint. 03   Choreographer: Janet Craft

Resident Designer for Emerson Stage

- **Drama: "Duchess of Malfi"**   **Producer: Emerson Stage**
  Semel Theatre, Fall 04   Director: Maureen Shea
- **Musical: "Pippin"**   **Producer: Emerson Stage**
  Majestic Theatre, Spring 04   Director. Stephen Terrell
- **Dance: "Something Old,**   **Producer: Emerson Stage**
  Something New"**
  Majestic Theatre, Winter 04   Director: Janet Craft
- **Musical: "Of Thee I Sing"**   **Producer: Emerson Stage.**
  Studio Theater, Spring 03   Director: Thomas DeFrantz
- **Dance: Spring Concert**   **Producers: Emerson Stage/Prometheus**
  Majestic Theater: Winter 02   Choreographers: Janet Craft, Sean Curran
  (*Former Dance Umbrella*), Tommy Nebblett (*Prometheus Dance Co.*)

Figure 11.1
(cont.)

Related Experience

1995-2003 Costume Design Professor and Area Head

- Professor Costume Design I and II, Fashion History and Costume Construction.
- Costume Area Head and Costume Design Thesis Tutor.

1995-2003 Operations Management

- Emerson College: Manage Departmental Accounts, Book-Keeping and Budget Reports for the Department's Chair.
- Boston University Division of Graduate Medical Services: Design of Academic-Administrative Space for the Mental Health and Behavioral Medicine Program.
- Bowdoin College: Design of Operation Systems for the Dance Theater Department.

Community Service

- USITT (United States Institute of Theater Technology) 2004, Portfolio Review Panels Design Chair for the Costume Commisison.
- USITT (United States Institute of Theater Technolongy) 2003, Workshop Chair Portfolio 101, presentation techniques for Students, Teachers and Professionals – Power Point presentation for 250 participants.
- USITT (United states Institute of Theater Technology) 2001-2003, Volunteer for Portfolio Review Panels.

Education

- **MA.** Theater Education. Emerson College. Boston. 2002.
- **MSS.** Theology. PTS School of Philosophy. New England Chapter. 1999.
- **BFA.** Theatrical Design. New York University. New York City. 1985.
- **BFA Candidate:** Architecture. Universidad Central de Venezuela. Caracas. 1978-1981.
- **Other:**
  - Managing Accelerated Productivity. TIME/DESIGN Corporation. California. Presentational and Facilitating Skills. Insight Seminars International California. 1993.
  - English as a Second Language, A. L. I. at NYU, New York. 1982.

Figure 11.2
The information in this two-page résumé has been reworked and reformatted from columns to sentences (fragments). It still includes professional experience, resident design experience, related experience (teaching, management, community service), and education. Notice that on page one the name and title at the top of the page are still clearly legible—again, contact information is included and important memberships are highlighted. More credits have been added on both pages, and the format is consistent.

Rafael Jaen
Costume Designer
H (617) 451-1157 & W(617) 824-8359. Email: rafael_jaen@emerson.edu
Member of USA 829 Chapter 829 and USITT Costume Commission

Experience

Costume design and Manufacturing

- **Gluck's "Alceste". Opera Boston.** Majestic Theatre, Boston, Winter 05. Director: Brad Dalton
- **T. Williams "Glass Menagerie". Lyric Stage.** Lyric Stage, Boston, Winter 05. Director: Eric Engel
- **Shakespeare's "Merchant of Venice". Publick Theatre.** Charles Rvier, Sum. 04. Director: D. Arciniegas
- **M. Carr's "On Raftery's Hill". Sugan Theater Co.** Boston Center for the Arts, Sprg 03. Director: Eric Engel
- **"Triple Exposure" & "Free Fall". Ipswich Moving Co.** BCA, Boston, Wint. 03. Director: Janet Craft
- **L. Cohen's "Epic Proportions". Lyric stage.** Lyric Stage, Boston, Fall 02. Director: Davis Robinson
- **D. Thomas' "Under Milkwood". Ablaze Theater.** Tremont Theater, Boston, Sum 02. Director: Mitchell Sellers
- **Hutton's "Last Train to Nibroc". Coyote Theater.** Boston Playwrights Th., Sum 01. Director: Maureen Shea
- **Pageant: "The Inspired Garden". MA Horticultural Society.** Bay Expo Center, Prev. March 01

Resident Designer for Emerson Stage

- **Drama: "Duchess of Malfi".** Semel Theatre, Fall 04. Director: Maureen Shea
- **Musical: "Pippin".** Majestic Theatre, Spring 04. Director: Stephen Terrell
- **Dance: "Something Old, Something New".** Majestic Theatre, Winter 04. Director: Janet Craft
- **Musical: "Of Thee I Sing".** Studio Theater, Spring 03. Director: Thomas DeFrantz
- **Dance: Spring Concert. Co-Producers: Prometheus Dance.** Majestic Theater, Winter 02. Choreographers: Janet Craft, Sean Curran (*Former Dance Umbrella*), Tommy Nebblett (*Prometheus Dance co.*)
- **Children's: "The Little Prince".** Majestic Theater, Fall 2001. Director: Robert Colby.
- **Musical: "Children of Eden". Co-Producers: MTS.** Majestic Theater, Spring 01. Director: Leo Nickole

Figure 11.2
(cont.)

1995-2003 Costume Design Professor and Area Head

- Professor Costume Design and II, Fashion History and Costume Construction.
- Costume Area Head and Costume Design Thesis Tutor.

Community Service

- USITT (United States Institute of Theater Technology) 2004, Portfolio Review Panels Design Chair for the Costume Commisison.
- USITT (United states institute of Theater Technology) 2003. Workshop Chair: Portfolio 101, presentation techniques for Students, Teachers and Professionals – Power Point presentation for 250 participants.
- USITT (United states Institute of Theater Technology) 2001-2003, Volunteer for Portfolio Review Panels.

Education

- **MA.** Theater Education. Emerson College. Boston. 2002.
- **MSS.** Theology. PTS School of Philosophy. New England Chapter. 1999.
- **BFA.** Theatrical Design. New York University. New York City. 1985.
- **BFA Candidate:** Architecture. Universidad Central de Venezuela. Caracas. 1798-1981.
- **Other:**
  - Managing Accelerated Productivity. TIME/DESIGN Corporation. California. 1992-93.
  - Presentational and Facilitating Skills. Insight Seminars International. California. 1993.
  - English as a Second Language, A. L. I. at NYU, New York. 1982.

Figure 11.3
The paper color, fonts, and graphics of a résumé must photocopy well in black and white when copies of it are made.

Rafael Jaen
Costume Designer
H (617) 451-1157 & W(617) 824-8359. Email: rafael_jaen@emerson.edu
Member of USA 829 Chapter 829 and USITT Costume Commission

Experience

Costume Design and Manufacturing

- **Gluck's "Alceste". Opera Boston.** Majestic Theatre, Boston, Winter 05. Director: Brad Dalton
- **T. Williams "Glass Menagerie". Lyric Stage.** Lyric Stage, Boston, Winter 05. Director: Eric Engel
- **Shakespeare's "Merchant of Venice". Publick Theatre.** Charles River, Sum. 04. Director: D. Arciniegas
- **M. Carr's "On Raftery's Hill". Sugan Theater Co.** Boston Center for the Arts, Sprg 03. Director: Eric Engel
- **"Triple Exposure" & "Free Fall". Ipswich Moving Co.** BCA, Boston, Wint. 03. Director: Janet Craft
- **L. Cohen's "Epic Proportions". Lyric Stage.** Lyric Stage, Boston, Fall 02. Director: Davis Robinson
- **D. Thomas' "Under Milkwood". Ablaze Theater.** Tremont Theater, Boston, Sum 02. Director: Mitchell Sellers
- **Hutton's "Last Train to Nibroc". Coyote Theater.** Boston Playwrights Th., Sum 01. Director: Maureen Shea
- **Pageant: "The Inspired Garden". MA Horticultural Society.** Bay Expo Center, Prev. March 01

Resident Designer for Emerson Stage

- **Drama: "Duchess of Malfi".** Semel Theatre, Fall 04. Director: Maureen Shea
- **Musical: "Pippin".** Majestic Theatre, Spring 04. Director: Stephen Terrell
- **Dance: "Something Old, Something New".** Majestic Theatre, Winter 04. Director: Janet Craft
- **Musical: "Of Thee I Sing".** Studio Theater, Spring 03. Director: Thomas DeFrantz
- **Dance: Spring Concert. Co-Producers: Prometheus Dance.** Majestic Theater. Winter 02. Choreographers: Janet Craft, Sean Curran (*Former Dance Umbrella*), Tommy Nebblett (*Prometheus Dance Co.*)
- **Children's "The Little Prince".** Majestic Theater, Fall 2001. Director: Robert Colby.
- **Musical: "Children of Eden". Co-Producers: MTS.** Majestic Theater, Spring 01. Director: Leo Nickole

3. Cards should minimally list the designer or technician's name, field of expertise, telephone number, and e-mail; the card can also list key affiliations and provide a business address.
4. Designers and technicians should always carry some business cards with them so they can be made available as needed.
5. Designers and technicians should always be prepared to exchange business cards in informal meetings and settings.
6. Designers and technicians need to update their roller deck on a regular basis, adding new business contacts and potential employers to their contact list. Acquiring business cards from prospective employers will help this task.

Rafael Jaen
Costume Design

Phone: (123) 456-7890.
Email: jaen@web.net
Member USA 829 & USITT
www.jaencostumes.net

Figure 11.4
(a) This business card includes some original artwork and color choices that suggest the style and expertise of the cardholder. Always make sure the graphics complement the written information rather than overwhelm it.

Rafael Jaen

Costume Designer

www.jaencostumes.net

Phone: (123) 456-7890. Email: jaen@web.net
Member of USA 829 Chapter 829
& USITT Costume Commission

Figure 11.4 (cont.)
(b) This simple business card mirrors the résumé featured earlier. It uses the same font style and color.

We have the case, the materials, and the résumé—where to now?

WORKBOOK: RÉSUMÉ PLANNING WHAT INFORMATION WOULD I LIKE TO INCLUDE IN MY RÉSUMÉ AND HOW SHOULD I FORMAT IT?

Chapter 12

Résumé, Curriculum Vitae, and Business Card Do's and Don'ts

A résumé is in many ways a work of art; it requires skill acquired by practice, learning, and observation. It also requires a conscious use of creative imagination—especially in the production of its aesthetic. The following excerpt from *The Pathfinder: How to Choose or Change Your Career for a Lifetime of Satisfaction and Success* by Nicholas Lore (Fireside, 1998; http://www.rockportinstitute.com/resumes.html) helps illustrate my theory.

From *The Pathfinder: How to Choose or Change Your Career for a Lifetime of Satisfaction and Success*

by Nicholas Lore

It is a mistake to think of your résumé as a history of your past, as a personal statement or as some sort of self expression. Sure, most of the content of any résumé is focused on your job history. But write from the intention to create interest, to persuade the employer to call you. If you write with that goal, your final product will be very different than if you write to inform or catalog your job history. Most people write a résumé because everyone knows that you have to have one to get a job. They write their résumé grudgingly, to fulfill this obligation. Writing the résumé is only slightly above filling out income tax forms in the hierarchy of worldly delights. If you realize that a great résumé can be your ticket to getting exactly the job you want, you may be able to muster some genuine enthusiasm for creating a real masterpiece, rather than the feeble products most people turn out.

Questions a Résumé Has to Answer

1. What key qualifications will the employer be looking for?
2. What qualifications that you possess will be most important to them?
3. Which of these are your greatest strengths?
4. What are the highlights of your career to date that should be emphasized?
5. What should be de-emphasized?
6. What things about you and your background make you stand out?
7. What are your strongest areas of skill and expertise? Knowledge? Experience?
8. What are some other skills you possess—perhaps more auxiliary skills?
9. What are characteristics you possess that make you a strong candidate? (Things like "innovative, hard-working, strong interpersonal skills, ability to handle multiple projects simultaneously under tight deadlines.")
10. What are the three or four things you feel have been your greatest accomplishments?
11. What was produced as a result of your greatest accomplishments?
12. Can you quantify the results you produced in numerical or other specific terms?
13. What were the two or three accomplishments of that particular job?
14. What were the key skills you used in that job? What did you do in each of those skill areas?
15. What sorts of results are particularly impressive to people in your field?
16. What results have you produced in these areas?
17. What are the "buzz words" that people in your field expect you to use in lieu of a secret club handshake, which should be included in your résumé?

During my many years of reviewing résumés at USITT (and other venues), plus researching effective ways to use them, I have observed some simple guidelines that will prove helpful in developing a résumé.

◼ DO'S

1. Do always include your contact information at the top of your résumé—especially your e-mail address and business telephone number.
2. Do remember to include your expertise as part of the title so your résumé can be archived properly. It is all right to have different résumés with different titles for different skills.
3. Do be sure that the identification, title, and contact information on the top of your résumé match the information on your business card. It is best if the font and style match, as well.
4. Do remember that a clear presentation and good grammar and spelling will always help make a good impression. Be sure to proofread your documents before making many copies.
5. Do avoid typos and misspellings of names of contributors, directors, etc.
6. When preparing a digital résumé file, do make sure it is in a Microsoft® Word format so it can be attached to an e-mail and opened easily by a prospective employer. Be sure to label the file with your name.
7. Do be aware that most employers prefer to read information in chronological order. Include your title on the job, the venue, show, director, etc.—whatever is relevant.
8. Do be sure that the number of pages corresponds with your years of experience. The consensus seems to be to keep the résumé between one page (less experience) and three pages (more experience).
9. Do save more detailed information for your curriculum vitae, such as community service, courses taught, or juried articles.

◼ DON'TS

1. Don't ever describe your experience inaccurately or alter show credits; such oversights may be interpreted as lies.
2. Don't design artsy layouts or overwhelming designs that will not copy well; always make a test run to see how it looks when photocopied or how easy it is to e-mail and open the file.
3. Don't fill the résumé with unnecessary information regarding hobbies, personal philosophies, and such; the résumé is simply an organized summary of your experience and education and serves as a tool for matching you to a job.

Part IV

Portfolio Maintenance and Next Steps

Chapter 13

Establishing Goals and Reviewing, Choosing, and Updating Work

When I started to collect materials for this book I wanted to be able to offer different options to readers planning on developing and maintaining their portfolios. We can establish goals and review our objectives, but we still have to choose the work that best represents us and update the portfolio often. Because no rules are set in stone, I have suggested some common guidelines or points that design–tech professionals need to think about. In this chapter, I provide input from two of my colleagues and add my own "teaching points" to help explain the planning and development process.

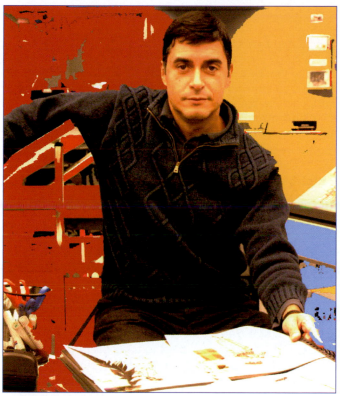

How I Set Up My Portfolio and Why

by Anthony R. Phelps

My portfolio is a heavy, large case. I chose this for two reasons: First, I was tired of having my wimpy vinyl portfolio cases destroyed at the airport on the conveyer belt, as well as the contents inside; second, I wanted a larger format to display my work. I have approximately 14 portfolio plates, that are 20 × 30″ and the photographs are mounted on matboard. I chose this because the matboard can withstand abuse and is easy to come by. Each 20 × 30″ portfolio plate contains pictures, drafting, drawings, and research materials for a particular show. Sometimes I use two plates to present a show. I never present all 14 plates during an interview. I choose the plates and productions that I feel show me in the best light to the employer; the other plates I hold in reserve for another interview or if the interviewer wants to see more.

◼ TEACHING POINT 1: THE CARRYING CASE

- Choose a case that will hold and protect your work.
- If you travel a lot, choose a sturdy case that is easy to carry.
- Choose the display technique that best suits your style.
- Be aware of the materials that you need for a basic layout (e.g., double-sided tape, rubber cement, matboard, portfolio pages) (Figure 13.1).
- Make sure you always have plenty of layout materials available.
- Plan all pages, beginning with your basic display technique and layout.

How I Set Up My Portfolio and Why (Cont.)

by Anthony R. Phelps

The materials on the plates vary from show to show. All plates have at least one 8 × 10″ photograph of the production and several smaller photographs, showing both full-stage and detail shots of the production. I include on several plates some research materials that influenced the design: a painting that I took colors from or a piece of furniture that we replicated. I also like to show bits of my drafting so you can have a better understanding of the stage and objects on it while looking at the production photographs. The drafting mounted to the portfolio plate is either shrunk down to a smaller scale or is just part of the original drafting, such as a detail of a wall. I have full drafting plates for several shows with me in the portfolio in their original format on 24 × 36″ paper, so if someone wants to see what the light plot or ground plan really looked like and what their shop could expect from me, I can show them. I do not carry the draftings for every show in my portfolio, as most people are not that interested in your drafting to see pages and pages of it. I feel it is only necessary to show a couple of shows with all of the draftings to prove that I can produce the necessary drawings for my job.

Figure 13.1
The author assembling his portfolio case and making decisions. He observes: "Be aware of the materials that you need for a basic layout (e.g., double-sided tape, rubber cement, matboard, portfolio pages)." (Photographs by Ariel Heller.)

▰ TEACHING POINT 2: FEATURED WORKS

- Include research materials to inform the process and choices made.
- Include written paragraphs or a concept narrative to explain the project (when needed).
- Include good-quality photographs in different sizes. Be sure to include a few 8.5 × 11″ prints (Figure 13.2).
- Shrink drafting and CAD drawings or include parts of the original size plans next to the fully realized projects.
- Be sure your materials showcase your various talents.

How I Set Up My Portfolio and Why (Cont.)

by Anthony R. Phelps

The major drawback of my portfolio is its size and weight, which is also why I like my portfolio. This portfolio is great for larger interview settings with several people. I can present it a plate at a time or set it up as a display and let people ask questions if the interview is less formal. When I need to do a smaller one-on-one interview, I use a smaller portfolio that I can fit easily on someone's desk.

▰ TEACHING POINT 3: PORTFOLIO SIZE

- Determine the appropriate portfolio size based on the interview setting; larger portfolios work best with large groups.
- Plan to have more than one portfolio if you will be interviewing in different settings, taking into consideration the portability and efficiency of the case.
- Make color copies and reduce your samples for use in multiple portfolios.
- Plan to have a digital portfolio or CD containing samples of your work that can be mailed or included in promotional materials.
- Remember that professional web pages can be used as alternative portfolios that any interested party can preview.

Words of Wisdom

Donna Meester, an Assistant Professor in the Department of Theatre and Dance at the University of Alabama, is head of the M.F.A. and undergraduate Costume Design and Production program. She writes: "*Process* and *collaboration* are two terms that are incredibly important when talking about the relationships between directors and designers. When looking at a portfolio, the reviewer will be looking not only at the quality of the art but also whether or not it communicates a process. Is there evidence of collaboration? In addition to displaying the final sketch and production photographs, research, notes, thumbnails, and any other additional information are welcome to see in a portfolio.

(Continued)

Figure 13.2
The author trying different configurations. He recommends: "Include good-quality sketches and photographs in different sizes." (Photographs by Ariel Heller.)

Figure 13.3
The author uses a carrying case size that allows him to present his work with confidence. He says: "Determine the appropriate portfolio size based on the interview setting; larger portfolios work best with large groups." (Photograph by Ariel Heller.)

"Paper and choice of media are important choices. A heavy, dark show probably is not best represented with a light, soft media on clean white paper; for example, Shakespeare's 'Titus Andronicus' is a dark show, best presented with dark, gritty medium on dark gritty paper. Always include photographs of the final product. While backstage costume shots are nice, particularly because they are often closer and clearer than an onstage shot, people looking at a portfolio want to see onstage shots. These tell many things: the quality of the overall production, how things work together on stage, if they look on stage as good as they do in the sketches or backstage, along with any number of other stories!"

TEACHING POINT 4: COMMUNICATING PROCESS

- Include research materials and other pertinent materials that show evidence of collaboration (*e.g.*, color palette of the other designers).
- Make sure your layout materials are congruent with the style of the play and they evoke the emotions, qualities, and actions of the show (*e.g.*, dark, gritty paper for a dark, gory show).
- Include backstage shots when they inform the process, but remember that what the reviewers are looking for is the final product.
- Let the page layout tell the story; let your visuals speak for themselves.

Figure 13.4
The author uses a medium-size case to present to a large group; all support materials are included in the final layout. He says: "Make sure your layout materials are congruent with the style of the play and they evoke the emotions, qualities, and actions of the show (e.g., dark, gritty paper for a dark, gory show)." (Photograph by Ariel Heller.)

Words of Wisdom (Cont.)

Donna Meester continues: "Sometimes work is included because the style and genre of the show are quite different from other shows featured in the portfolio. For large shows, particularly those with identifiable groups, one way to organize the presentation is by groupings of such groups. These pages can be presented in a portfolio with the research and photograph pages, with the painted sketches positioned next to the group they belong with. Another presentation would be to have all of the research or photograph pages together followed by the complete set of sketches. Don't feel compelled to include one sketch per page. If more than one fits, use the space! While research is important for the designer to base designs on and to help communicate ideas to the director, it is also often necessary to share this information with the shop. Research can be attached to sketches, drafting, etc., or can stand on its own. Sometimes a designer wants to keep the show production bible (binder) intact. Regardless of the method of presentation, everything should be organized. Don't be afraid to show where ideas began. Include everything that helped you get to the final product."

Figure 13.5
Sometimes a short design concept or a descriptive paragraph can help explain the visual content of sketches and graphics.

TEACHING POINT 5: FEATURED WORKS

- Organize the work in the portfolio to demonstrate variety and range of artistry.
- For a large show, group sketches of different sizes to fit the portfolio page.
- Remember that the order of presentation is important: research, sketches, and then final product.
- Save production books if they demonstrate added expertise and informs the process.
- Keep production books neatly organized for easy reading during a review.

Figure 13.6
For a relaxed setting, the author chooses a vertical layout to present a well-polished portfolio. He observes: "Remember that the order of presentation is important: research, sketches, and then final product." (Photograph by Ariel Heller.)

I understand the teaching points, and I am ready to start my planning. What steps can I take to apply these teaching points?

WORKBOOK: APPLYING TEACHING POINTS
WHAT TEACHING POINTS CAN I APPLY IN
DEVELOPING AND MAINTAINING MY
PORTFOLIO?

Chapter 14
Self-Assessment

Developing and maintaining a design–tech portfolio can be a structured and well-organized job; however, we have to remember that in its very nature it is more of an organic process than a scientific one. This is why it is important to assess where you are in the development of your showcase on an ongoing basis; you need to integrate feedback and keep your perspective as you move forward. As you archive your work, you should consider what to put aside for the portfolio and do some loose planning for when it is time to update it. Sometimes you might be inspired to do so by your internal clock or time off, a job interview might come along, you might be invited to present at a conference, or you might have to meet timelines and requirements that organizations will impose.

THE BASICS OF A SELF-EVALUATION

In Chapter 9, I introduced the idea of self-evaluation. My findings suggest that after an interview it is important to act on any feedback in order to prepare for future opportunities. Because designers and technicians can be their own worst critics, it is important to do a self-assessment in a self-supporting, honest, and caring way. A neutral evaluation would take into consideration the panelists' feedback, future goals, and the next steps to take. A self-assessment questionnaire would include questions about style, voice, rapport, and content. These are some examples:

1. *Style*—Was my personal grooming and appearance favorable, average, or unfavorable? Why? What are the next steps?
2. *Voice*—Were my volume and articulation favorable, average, or unfavorable? Why? What are the next steps?
3. *Rapport*—Were the conversations empathetic? Did I listen well? Did I give comprehensive answers? Was this aspect favorable, average, or unfavorable? Why? What are the next steps?
4. *Content*—Were the preparation, research, work samples, and subject knowledge sufficient? Was this aspect favorable, average, or unfavorable? Why? What are the next steps?

We can all agree that it is important to self-evaluate after an interview in order to act on the feedback received, but we have to be discriminating and clear about what feedback we choose to integrate or eliminate. The feedback you receive might be good for applying to a school program but it may not work as well when applying for a position with a professional organization or for a teaching job. It is important that we self-assess to determine our next steps based on our career concept and our blueprint for short-term goals (see Chapter 15).

THE COMPREHENSIVE SELF-EVALUATION

The following is a workbook that I have developed for the purpose of self-assessment; it contains basic questions or prompters that help clarify the process. I suggest that you refer to these questions as you go through your archives and take notice of what requires attention, then take care of your portfolio and go back to your career master plan!

Workbook: The Self-Assessment Questionnaire

Rate yourself as you work through these questions, then choose a strategy for each item that requires attention.

My Portfolio Case

- Is my portfolio case clean, appropriate, and professional looking? Is it easy to handle?
Rating: 1 [ ] 2 [ ] 3 [ ] 4 [ ] 5 [ ]   (1, needs improvement; 5, excellent!)
Strategy: Does this item require attention? What steps will I take to take care of this?

My Portfolio Inside (Supplies)

- Are the sheets holders in good shape, clean, and smudge free? Do I have enough extra sheets?
Rating: 1 [ ] 2 [ ] 3 [ ] 4 [ ] 5 [ ]   (1, needs improvement; 5, excellent!)
Strategy: Does this item require attention? What steps will I take to take care of this?

My Portfolio Content

- Is the first page well designed?
Rating: 1 [ ] 2 [ ] 3 [ ] 4 [ ] 5 [ ]   (1, needs improvement; 5, excellent!)
Strategy: Does this item require attention? What steps will I take to take care of this?
- Do I have an ample supply of updated résumés and business cards?
Rating: 1 [ ] 2 [ ] 3 [ ] 4 [ ] 5 [ ]   (1, needs improvement; 5, excellent!)
Strategy: Does this item require attention? What steps will I take to take care of this?
- Do I have clear transitions between projects, with continuous horizontal or vertical layouts?
Rating: 1 [ ] 2 [ ] 3 [ ] 4 [ ] 5 [ ]   (1, needs improvement; 5, excellent!)
Strategy: Does this item require attention? What steps will I take to take care of this?
- Do I have careful project organization with comprehensive displays of the process, including research, plans, and rough and final sketches?
Rating: 1 [ ] 2 [ ] 3 [ ] 4 [ ] 5 [ ]   (1, needs improvement; 5, excellent!)
Strategy: Does this item require attention? What steps will I take to take care of this?
- Is my translation of a concept to design choices and palettes clear? Do I have good attention to details?
Rating: 1 [ ] 2 [ ] 3 [ ] 4 [ ] 5 [ ]   (1, needs improvement; 5, excellent!)
Strategy: Does this item require attention? What steps will I take to take care of this?
- Is my sketch quality good?
- *Rating:* 1 [ ] 2 [ ] 3 [ ] 4 [ ] 5 [ ]   (1, needs improvement; 5, excellent!)
Strategy: Does this item require attention? What steps will I take to take care of this?
- Are things clearly labeled, is the color media fixed properly, do my sketches need to be bordered or matted?
Rating: 1 [ ] 2 [ ] 3 [ ] 4 [ ] 5 [ ]   (1, needs improvement; 5, excellent!)
Strategy: Does this item require attention? What steps will I take to take care of this?
- Do I have final renderings next to production photographs? Are the photographs good quality? Are the photographs true to the production?
Rating: 1 [ ] 2 [ ] 3 [ ] 4 [ ] 5 [ ]   (1, needs improvement; 5, excellent!)
Strategy: Does this item require attention? What steps will I take to take care of this?

My Portfolio Back Pocket

- Do I have any necessary production books and paperwork?
Rating: 1 [ ] 2 [ ] 3 [ ] 4 [ ] 5 [ ]   (1, needs improvement; 5, excellent!)
Strategy: Does this item require attention? What steps will I take to take care of this?

Me, the Presenter

- How about my grooming, presence, and appearance—do I have the proper attire for an interview? Do I need a haircut?
Rating: 1 [ ] 2 [ ] 3 [ ] 4 [ ] 5 [ ]   (1, needs improvement; 5, excellent!)
Strategy: Does this item require attention? What steps will I take to take care of this?
- How are my voice projection, listening skills, and idea articulation? Do I need to rehearse prior to my interview? Am I missing something on paper (such as properly labeled projects) that could facilitate my verbal presentation?
Rating: 1 [ ] 2 [ ] 3 [ ] 4 [ ] 5 [ ]   (1, needs improvement; 5, excellent!)
Strategy: Does this item require attention? What steps will I take to take care of this?

(Continued)

- Is my verbal presentation clear and to the point? Does it match my organization (beginning, middle, end; charts and forms)?

Rating: 1 [ ]   2 [ ]   3 [ ]   4 [ ]   5 [ ]   (1, needs improvement; 5, excellent!)

Strategy: Does this item require attention? What steps will I take to take care of this?

Chapter 15

Planning for the Next Job

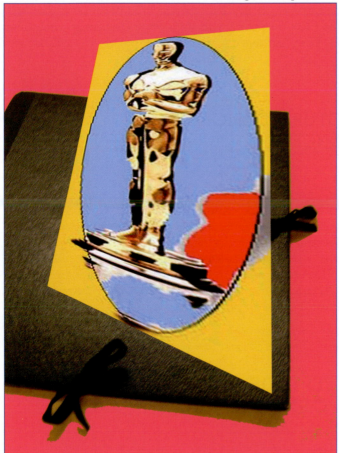

There are two sayings in theater that have stayed with me through the years: "No matter how good you are, you still have to audition" and "You are only as good as your last project." We are no different from professionals in other fields, and we share the same concerns regarding advancement, opportunity, better pay, recognition, getting a new job, growing in the job, making changes, leaving a legacy, planning for retirement, etc. How many times did you find yourself competing for a job that you knew you were best qualified for but did not get? How many times have you had a fantastic process working on a show and yet have received a bad critic's review? (Producers say that it doesn't matter, but we wonder if they will call us again.) Or, have you had an interview at a college where the reviewers did not think your body of work was impressive enough? Or, have you expected a raise or bonus that never came?

Our field is very competitive, and it is sometimes challenging to break into new territory due to demanding schedules, constant deadlines, and closed networks of people. Sometimes resources are limited, creating a scarcity mentality. How do we keep ourselves prepared for the next audition, and how do we overcome a bad project? The answer is to remain inspired, marching forward with a clear vision and a plan.

In a profession that is highly creative, it is important that we take the time to map out our future, to come up with a "career concept" (or vision) and to create a blueprint (or next steps) for what we want to do next. We need to produce, market, and take our own show on the road!

PUTTING IT TOGETHER

The process of preparing, developing, and maintaining a portfolio can help us set goals for the next step in our career development. It is important to allow time in our schedule for portfolio maintenance. The portfolio will inform how we are doing. What information can we get from reviewing our projects? It could be as simple as realizing that we need to get more pages or as challenging as adding new state-of-the-art production work. There are two basic concepts to consider in our planning: (1) a vision of the big picture, what I call the *career concept*, and (2) the next steps or short-term goals, which I refer to as a *blueprint*. In my experience, this process works best when it is fluid; we need to balance it with life's other demands, including our everyday routines. Keep an eye on your goals, but do not obsess too much about them.

THE BIG PICTURE: DESIGN–TECH CAREER CONCEPT

Back in the mid- to late-1980s, I had the opportunity to take various business courses at Boston University. Since then, one thing I learned that has remained with me even today is that business planning mirrors (in many ways) the process of designing and producing a show. First, we need to have a vision that addresses what we ultimately want to achieve; this vision becomes the concept. This concept can include all sorts of things, from practical to philosophical. By answering the question "Where do we want to be in five years?" we can work our way back to determining the steps we must take now.

YOUR CONCEPT: IDENTIFYING PRACTICAL CONSIDERATIONS

First we have to come up with a list of five to ten accomplishments that we would like to achieve in five years; I call this the *wish list* (see box). Then, just as in a production, we have to consider the interpersonal relations, budgets, timelines, venues, and script needs that will get us there. It is important to take time to brainstorm, take notes, and make lists. The advantage of this approach to career planning is that we are both producer and director; therefore, the final choices are ours!

The Wish List

The wish list can include anything from earning a better income to receiving awards, from getting a color marker collection of 150 colors to buying a larger drafting table, from owning a scenic company to having a staff of 20 workers, from having a retirement account to getting comprehensive health insurance. This is perhaps the most difficult part of this planning process; we are so used to supporting the vision of others that coming up with our own may feel alien to us. I say write your list anyway, being sure to include both big and small items.

Interpersonal Relations

Interpersonal relations refers to your network of people. Our field survives on teamwork; therefore, it is important to realize who is on our team as we plan. A list of such team members would include key people who could become resources when and if the need arises. It would also include friends, colleagues, newspaper critics, independent press reviewers, specialty magazine editors, organizations (regional and national), unions and guilds, group insurance companies, vendors, computer technicians, etc. You do not have to anticipate every need here; instead, consider what is key for the first year. For example, if you want to be designing for a LORT theater in five years, it would help to get into the United Scenic Artist Union within three years.

The Budget Matter

Budget obviously relates to income, but it could also address such things as scholarship opportunities, grants, renting a studio with other design–tech folks, or even recycling materials. It is important to be creative and daring when thinking about money. Assess what kind of income you need to take care of your living expenses and financial goals. Do you need to acquire new skills in order to get better pay? Do you need to change companies? Do you need to branch out into an allied field? Remember that we can be very resourceful when putting together a show and this is a five-year plan, so every day will bring you closer to realizing your career design.

Venues

Venues refers to geography, environment, space, and location. Do you need to live and work in a warm area, or does your family need to be

(Continued)

located in a certain area of the country? Do you aspire to work in a shop that is OSHA compliant? Would you like to have a larger studio with better equipment? Would you like to be closer to the stores that sell the supplies you need for your work? Do you want to be the technical director for a drama department in an elementary school in Vermont?

Your Script, Your Needs

Because this plan is self-scripted, you will find that as you put your big ideas and vision on paper some other considerations will arise—I call these the *script needs*. The design–tech career concept will have to be revised and updated continually, just like a show. Suppose you want to be on Broadway in five years but you just started your undergraduate degree; in this case, your initial goal might be to get into the proper union and work as an assistant. Or, suppose you want to receive an important award that will look impressive in a promotion and tenure file; in this case, it might be better to develop a more general goal of "earning professional recognition" rather than "winning an Oscar." Perhaps it is unlikely that you will be awarded a Tony, an Emmy or an Oscar next year, but you could enter a juried event (writing a design–tech paper, sharing some new technology, etc.). Sometimes we need to translate some of the bigger, more specific goals into more attainable, general goals. What is important is to continue moving in the general direction of your plan.

THE SMALL STEPS: YOUR BLUEPRINT FOR SHORT-TERM GOALS

Once you have come up with a design–tech career concept, you need to look at your portfolio and résumés to determine what short-term goals to put into place. This is the process I refer to as developing the *design–tech blueprint*; it is the "nuts and bolts" of the overall planning process. It will help you gather up the loose ends and set short-term goals. I keep a list of short-term goals in a visible place that I can refer to as a reminder. In our field we tend to create what we focus on—same with the design–tech career concept. It is important to let the process be fluid and balance it with life's other demands. The blueprint includes five to ten short-term goals. The objective is to accomplish as many of these goals as possible within a chosen time frame; some people work well setting quarterly goals, while others might prefer to give themselves a year. The blueprint might include such items as updating portfolio materials, developing new works, promotion and marketing, education and training, etc.

Questions to Ask When Creating a Blueprint List

- Is my portfolio case in good shape? Does it look professional?
- Is my portfolio up-to-date? Do I need to add my last few shows?
- Which work should I keep in or add to the portfolio? What work should go in the archives?
- Do I have all the production sketches, swatches, photographs, programs, etc., that I need to add to new portfolio pages?
- Will I need a digital portfolio to apply for graduate school or as part of my promotional package?
- Are my résumé and business cards up-to-date? Do I have at least two dozen copies available with my portfolio?
- Do I need to mail my résumé to companies in another state?
- Should I create a web page for my business? If I have a website, is it up-to-date?
- Do I have press reviews and promotional materials? Do I need to add mention of an award in my portfolio?
- Do I need new or different projects to expand my portfolio?

The goal of the blueprint is to help maintain and develop a portfolio that can assist you in achieving the larger concept or vision you hold for yourself as a professional in your field.

WORKBOOK: PLANNING THE NEXT JOB   WHEN REVIEWING BOTH THE DESIGN–TECH CONCEPT AND THE BLUEPRINT, IT IS IMPORTANT TO LOOK FOR INCONGRUENCE AND ELIMINATE ANYTHING THAT DOES NOT SUPPORT THE PLAN. JUST LIKE ON A SHOW, SOMETIMES PARTS GET CUT DUE TO TIME OR BUDGET RESTRAINTS. IT IS IMPORTANT TO ESTABLISH CLEAR AND OBTAINABLE GOALS. YOU CAN WRITE DOWN YOUR IDEAS AND BRAINSTORMS IN THIS WORKBOOK.

Chapter 16
Portfolio Do's and Don'ts

I n previous chapters we have read the guidelines that many experienced professionals and seasoned academicians recommend when developing a portfolio. While there are no hard-set rules some standards do apply. This section will look at some commonly accepted practices and things to avoid. These are the golden keys or the DO'S and the DON'T'S of portfolio development, presentation techniques, and marketing.

PORTFOLIO DEVELOPMENT DO'S AND DON'TS

DO'S

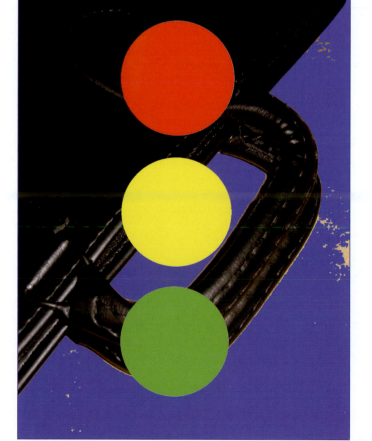

- Do include the materials needed to apply for a specific job. Most reviewers will say that a portfolio must be put together in such a way that it answers questions specific to its goals. A portfolio prepared to apply for graduate school will have to meet different expectations than one used to apply for a job as a designer or technician in regional theatre.
- Do start with your strongest produced work. For students, begin the portfolio with the strongest class projects, including art class projects, photography, etc. At the professional level, the same rule applies; always show only work that you feel confident about.

- Do include art projects at the end of the portfolio or in a separate binder if the portfolio is filled up with produced work and design–tech class projects.
- Do review the portfolio materials often so you are able to talk about your work from a number of different points of view (e.g., concepts, process, budget).
- Do include a piece of promotional material (a program or flyer, not reviews), as well as a minimum of one or two sketches and production photographs for each production being shown. Students should include class projects but at the end, not at the beginning, of the presentation.
- Do be sure that the sketch lettering is neat, that the edges are not ragged, that pastels are fixed, etc. Sketches, swatches, and research should be affixed to the portfolio pages.
- Do present projects in reverse chronological order, if that will be more effective; there is no rule stating that a portfolio has to be in any particular type of chronological order.
- Do be sure that draftings, blueprints, and CAD drawings are a readable size; photographs must be true to the stage color and contain detail.
- Do include sources and titles for research and reference materials.
- Do include dates and title pages for news and other media articles; the goal is to give reviewers as many contexts as possible so they can quickly understand the scale and venue of the work being presented.
- Do keep in mind that the layout and design of the portfolio pages are as important as the work itself; keep the principles of design in mind when planning your page layout and your rendering plates.

DON'TS

- Don't include badly organized materials, incomplete projects, and pages that must be turned a different way to view the various pictures.
- Don't spread too much information over too many pages; do not include the kitchen sink!
- Don't apologize for anything in your portfolio; if it requires an apology, it probably doesn't belong in it.
- Don't forget that, if your pictures don't look good, it doesn't matter how good your work looked in real life; become your own photographer.

DIGITAL PORTFOLIO DO'S AND DON'TS

There are some basic things to remember when planning and executing a digital portfolio to be stored on a CD or presented on a website. Always remember that the work should represent you and your skills above all.

DO'S

- Do ask for help from your computer wizard friends.
- Do save your work on a CD in a format compatible with both Macs and PCs.
- Do attach a written statement with your CD explaining the contents of the portfolio.
- Do choose the best images of completed projects, as well as media clips.

- Do look for website domain providers that offer templates that will help you design a professional-looking site.
- Do start your website with a few pages, keeping things simple and small.
- Do plan for easy and inexpensive maintenance.
- Do label things clearly and add notes as needed for instant gratification.

DON'TS

- Don't use low-quality photographs on your website or CD.
- Don't rely exclusively on scanning photographs; it is best to start with digital film.
- Don't retouch pictures (e.g., color correction) to the point where they no longer look like the staged production.
- Don't make the site all about flash and splash.
- Don't make the website so complicated that it takes a long time to load.
- Don't focus on the layout at the expense of the content.

THEATRE, TELEVISION, AND FILM PORTFOLIO PRESENTATION TECHNIQUES DO'S AND DON'TS

DO'S

- Do plan a beginning, a middle, and an end for the portfolio presentation.
- Do take time to meet the interviewers and establish eye contact.
- Do project your voice and speak clearly.
- Do remember good grooming and professional manners and appearance.
- Do review your portfolio materials often and always prior to your interview.
- Do plan a short summary for each project.
- Do make sure the portfolio layout is clear.
- Do make sure that project sequences do not compete with each other.
- Do make sure that projects are labeled and keyed properly.
- Do make sure to have source lists for research, materials, etc.
- Do have support materials in the back pocket.
- Do have updated résumés and business cards.

DON'TS

- Don't present a disorganized portfolio.
- Don't avoid looking at your interviewers.
- Don't look like you just finished pulling an all-nighter.
- Don't have bad grooming, including unkempt fingernails.
- Don't forget sketch labels or keys.
- Don't have different, competing projects adjacent to each other.
- Don't use bad photographs or incomplete research or sketches.
- Don't use loose pages.
- Don't end with a weak project.

- Don't forget to give credit to other artists' work featured with a project.
- Don't ignore questions or get defensive.
- Don't forget to distribute your résumé and business cards.

■ RESUME, CURRICULUM VITAE, AND BUSINESS CARDS DO'S AND DON'TS

During my many years of reviewing résumés at USITT (and other venues), plus researching effective ways to use them, I have observed some simple guidelines that will prove helpful in developing a résumé.

|DO'S

- Do always include your contact information at the top of your résumé—especially your e-mail address and business telephone number.
- Do remember to include your expertise as part of the title so your résumé can be archived properly. It is all right to have different résumés with different titles for different skills.
- Do be sure that the identification, title, and contact information on the top of your résumé match the information on your business card. It is best if the font and style match, as well.
- Do remember that a clear presentation and good grammar and spelling will always help make a good impression. Be sure to proofread your documents before making many copies.
- Do avoid typos and misspellings of names of contributors, directors, etc.
- When preparing a digital résumé file, do make sure it is in a Microsoft® Word format so it can be attached to an e-mail and opened easily by a prospective employer. Be sure to label the file with your name.
- Do be aware that most employers prefer to read information in chronological order. Include your title on the job, the venue, show, director, etc.—whatever is relevant.
- Do be sure that the number of pages corresponds with your years of experience. The consensus seems to be to keep the résumé between one page (less experience) and three pages (more experience).
- Do save more detailed information for your curriculum vitae, such as community service, courses taught, or juried articles.

|DON'TS

- Don't ever describe your experience inaccurately or alter show credits; such oversights may be interpreted as lies.
- Don't design artsy layouts or overwhelming designs that will not copy well; always make a test run to see how it looks when photocopied or how easy it is to e-mail and open the file.
- Don't fill the résumé with unnecessary information regarding hobbies, personal philosophies, and such; the résumé is simply an organized summary of your experience and education and serves as a tool for matching you to a job.

A theatrical design–tech portfolio is a showcase of a designer or technician's process, resourcefulness, and artistry. This showcase is key in opening new doors and getting into recognized colleges, obtaining scholarships, and getting new jobs in the field. Putting a portfolio together for presentation can seem like an impossible undertaking and it can be a time-consuming and challenging process, but I hope you keep finding this process useful, inspiring, and helpful!

Part V

Contributors

Chapter 17
Contributors

Many people contributed to this book—mentors, colleagues, students, academicians, freelancers, and professionals in allied fields. Their feedback was always helpful and encouraging. Each one of them shares my passion and love for design technology and believes in the importance of portfolio development in our field. In this chapter, I present their brief biographies with some credits, quotes, and samples.

APRIL BARTLETT, SCENIC DESIGNER

April Bartlett is a graduate student working on her M.F.A. at Carnegie Mellon, with a Scenic Design concentration; she received her B.F.A. in 2004 at Emerson College in Boston. Among her recognitions are an award for Meritorious Achievement in Scenic Design, American College Theatre Festival (2004); Who's Who Among American Students (2004); and the EVVY Award for Achievement in Scenic Design (2004).

April Bartlett's says: "Make your portfolio tell a story. You're not always there to talk about every page. You may only have a 15-minute interview slot; having your portfolio be able to speak for itself allows you to focus on answering the interviewer's questions. You've mapped out a book for yourself to read when showing your portfolio; instead of thinking about what you're going to say next, all you have to do is turn the page."

JESSICA CHAMPAGNE

Jessica Champagne is currently a first-year graduate costume design student at the University of California, Irvine; she graduated with a B.F.A. in 2005 in Design/Technology with a concentration in Costume Design from Emerson College in Boston. She won the 2004 ACTF Barbizon Design Award for Region I and attended URTA in 2005.

ARIKA COHEN

Arika Cohen graduated from Emerson College in Boston with a B.F.A. in Design–Technology (Scenic and Costumes) and a minor in Theatre Education. In 2005, while in the Boston area, Erica managed to combine teaching

Figure 17.1
Jessica Champagne's sketch for the character of Simon Bass in "The Shakespeare Stealer" (Emerson Stage, Boston, 2004).

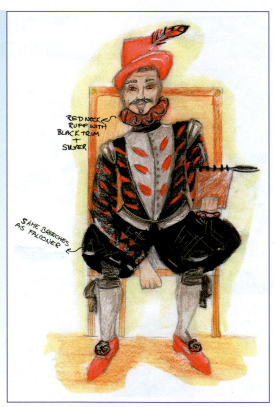

Figure 17.2
The act of presenting (illustration by Arika Cohen).

and design into her daily schedule. Her most recent works could be seen at productions of the Boston's Children Theatre.

ERIC CORNELL

Eric Cornell owns and operates Cornell Consulting, an arts management consulting business focused on aiding and establishing emerging companies and artists in New York, Boston, and Washington, D.C. Additionally, Eric has worked extensively throughout the country: on Broadway ("The Producers," "Hairspray"); off-Broadway ("Perfect Crime," "In the Air"); elsewhere in New York ("People Like Us" at NYMF); and at regional theatres (The Barn Theatre, Peterborough Players, American Repertory Theatre, Broad-

Figure 17.3
Eric Cornell's photograph of an aluminum portfolio case (see Figure 2.1).

way in Boston/Clear Channel Entertainment). Originally from Oklahoma, Eric received his B.A. in Theatre from Emerson College in Boston and now resides in New York, NY (www.ericcornell.com).

■ ANN CUDWORTH

Ann Cudworth has worked professionally in the four realms of set design: theatre, film, television, and virtual reality. In 1977, she started out by designing a production of "The Nutcracker" for the Lexington Ballet Company in Lexington, Kentucky. Shortly afterward, she designed shows for the MIT Shakespeare Ensemble with director Murray Biggs and at the Nucleo Ecclectico in Boston. When she moved to New York City in 1983 for graduate school, she worked on many student films and stage presentations for NYU and Columbia University. After graduation from NYU in 1986, she continued to work in the Art Department on feature films and commercials. By 1987, she was an art director for feature films shooting in New York. She then moved on to television, starting with soap operas. Ann holds the unusual distinction of designing four disasters for three different soap operas in one season. Eventually, this work led to a permanent freelance position with CBS in 1994. For the last 13 years, Ann has been a production designer for shows

Figure 17.4
Ann Cudworth's web page for virtual scenery.

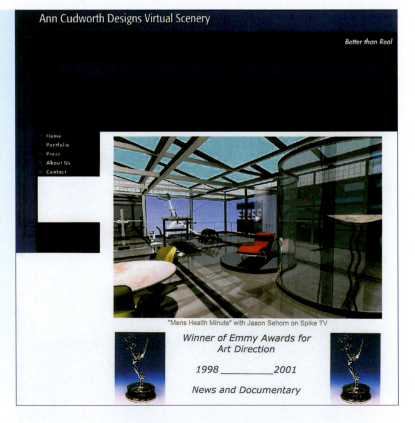

Figure 17.5
The author assembling his portfolio (photograph by Ariel Heller).

at CBS, such as "60 Minutes," "48 Hours," and special events programming. The creation of virtual scenic pieces for the 1994 election coverage started Ann's virtual set design career. Her current work can be seen on projects for "Market Watch" and CBS news promotions. She has won two Emmys, one for a real set and one for a virtual set.

ARIEL HELLER

Ariel Heller is a 2006 graduate of Emerson College in Boston, with a B.F.A. in Musical Theatre. He has also studied acting as an apprentice at Brown University's Trinity Repertory. A New Hampshire native, he has performed in regional theater, as well as at Boston's Majestic Theatre and the Boston Lyric Stage. His credits include "Guys and Dolls" (Harry the Horse), "Pippin" (Lewis), and "Urinetown, The Musical" (Ensemble). Ariel is also an avid photographer and a world-champion target archer.

WILLIAM GORDON HENSHAW

William Gordon Henshaw (M.F.A. in Drama from San Diego State University, 1996) is the resident costume designer at Henderson State University in Arkadelphia, Arkansas. William's awards include being a Kennedy Center American College Theater Festival Regional Costume Design Nominee, the Bernice Prisk award for Excellence in Theatrical Costuming, and the Wendell Johnson award for Excellence in Design. He is a member of national and regional chapters of the United States Institute for Theatre Technology (USITT).

Figure 17.6
William
Henshaw's
research plate for
"An American
Tragedy" (San
Diego State
University, 1996).

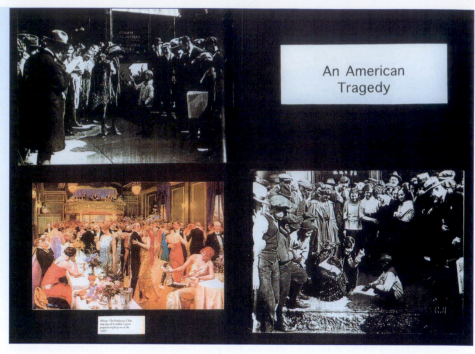

JANIE E. HOWLAND

Janie E. Howland is a scenic designer, a member of United Scenic Artists
Local 829, an Elliot Norton Award winner, and founding member of the Cyco
Scenic production company. She received her M.F.A. in Scenic Design from
Brandeis University in 1993 and her B.A. in Art History from the University
of Pennsylvania in 1987.

Figure 17.7
Janie Howland's
set for "Inherit the
Wind" at the
Wheelock Family
Theatre in Boston.

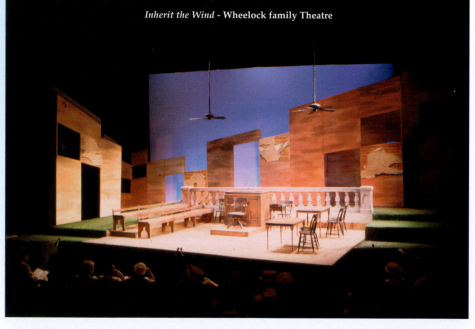

Figure 17.8
One of John Iacovelli's white models for "Casablanca, the Dance" produced by Warner Bros. Theatricals in 2005.

JOHN IACOVELLI

John Iacovelli has done theatrical set designs for Broadway and regional theatre productions, art direction and production design for television and film, and art direction and production design for videos and industrials. Some of his impressive career credits include set design for many Broadway productions (*e.g.*, "Peter Pan"), art direction for such television shows as "The Crosby Show," production design for "Resurrection Boulevard" and "Babylon 5," art direction for the film "Honey, I Shrunk the Kids," and industrial installations for the Summer 1996 Olympics and Disney.

Figure 17.9
Scenic shots from the Westport Country Playhouse production of "Member of the Wedding," for which Andrew Kirsch was responsible for scenic construction.

ANDREW KIRSCH

Andrew Kirsch earned his B.F.A. degree in Technical Theatre in 2006 from Emerson College in Boston. Andrew's photographs for this book arrived just as he completed technical direction for the Emerson Stage production of "Undiscovered Country." He spent the summer of 2005 as the Scenic Construction Intern for Westport Country Playhouse's 75th season and worked on "Dear Brutus" and "Journey's End" (directed by Gregory Boyd) and "Member of the Wedding" (directed by Joanne Woodward). Andrew's interest in theatre tech began at Camp Dudley in Westport, New York, when he was 8 years old.

KITTY LEECH

Kitty Leech has a M.F.A. in design from New York University's Tisch School of the Arts. Her costume design credits include seven companies of "Gross Indecency: The Three Trials of Oscar Wilde," including the original New York productions as well as productions in San Francisco, Los Angeles, Toronto, and London's West End. Other notable off-Broadway credits include "The Novelist: A Romantic Portrait of Jane Austen" by Howard Fast and "Goblin Market," for which she received a Maharam award nomination. Currently she is on the faculty at New York University's Tisch School of the Arts Drama Department and the Playwrights Horizons Theatre School. Kitty has reviewed hundreds of portfolios while chairing the Costume Design Exam Committee for the United Scenic Artists Local 829 (a committee she has served on since 1987) and also chairing the Young Master's Award Committee for the Theatre Development Fund's Irene Sharaff Awards. She has been a guest artist at the American International School in Salzburg, Austria, and a guest lecturer at The Parsons School of Design, Pratt Institute, and Lincoln Center Theatre.

Kitty Leech says: "Don't ever say anything negative or derogatory about another designer, director, or actor while you are discussing the work in your portfolio. Everyone in this business knows everyone else. If you found someone difficult to work with, just say that it was a 'challenge.' Everyone will know what you mean. We've all been there!"

ANDY LEVISS

Andy Leviss is a sound designer and nationally touring sound engineer. He earned his B.F.A. in Theatre Design/Technology at Emerson College. He won the 2003 EVVY Award for Outstanding Achievement in Sound Design and maintains the website OneFromTheRoad.com (Tools, Toys, and Tales for the Theatrical Technician).

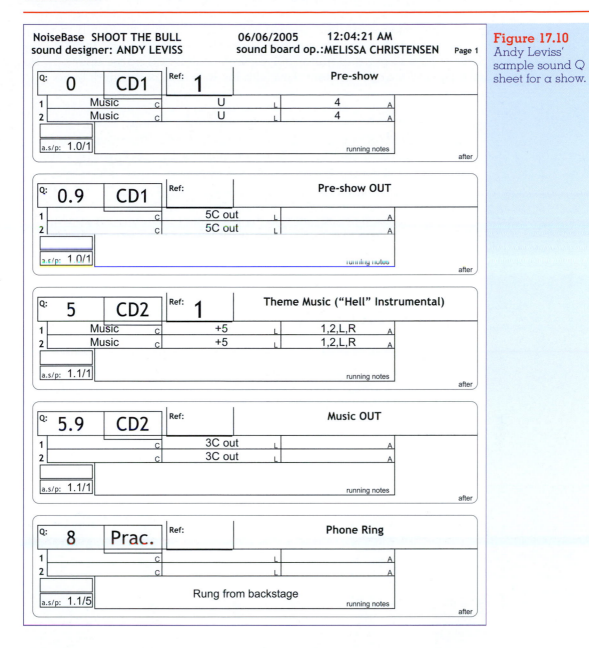

Figure 17.10
Andy Leviss' sample sound Q sheet for a show.

NICHOLAS LORE

Nicholas Lore is the founder of Rockport Institute, an international career consulting firm that has coached many thousands of clients through mid-career changes or first-time career decisions. He and his staff have worked with business executives, government officials, technical people, support staff, artists, musicians, and professionals in all fields. He has been commended for excellence by two U.S. presidents. As the director of Rockport Institute, he is a mentor to many of the most gifted career, personal, and business coaches around the world. Nicholas also serves as a personal consultant to CEOs who want their organizations filled with happy, committed, productive people. He has been a corporate CEO, manufacturing plant manager, entrepreneur, researcher in the field of psychology, market gardener, blues singer and guitar player, well driller, and newspaper boy. He lives by a lake under ancient oaks with his wife and best friend, Mitra.

Excerpt from Nicholas Lore's *The Pathfinder: How to Choose or Change Your Career for a Lifetime of Satisfaction and Success* (Fireside, 1998): "If you plan to have a deeply satisfying career, one that goes beyond the ordinary level of satisfaction and success most people accept, then it may be worth noticing that there seems to be a mechanism at work that tends to keep people stuck to the same spot on the flypaper of life. The better you are at unsticking the stuck, the more power you have to say how your life will be."

DONNA MEESTER

Donna Meester is an Assistant Professor in the Department of Theatre and Dance at the University of Alabama, where she is Head of the M.F.A. and undergraduate Costume Design and Production program. She has served as the Design Chair for the Kennedy Center American College Theatre Festival (Region VI) and is currently the Design Vice-Chair for Region IV. Donna is also an active member of the United States Institute for Theatre Technology (USITT) and the Southeastern Theatre Conference (SETC).

Figure 17.11 Donna Meester's portfolio page of costumes designed for "Twelfth Night" (University of Louisiana, Monroe).

Figure 17.12
Amanda Monteiro's costume portfolio page sample includes original sketches and production photos.

AMANDA MONTEIRO

In Amanda Monteiro's own words: "The privilege of working with Rafael opened doors I had never even contemplated. After beginning his first design class, a passion awoke that was never there before. Before I knew it, I had taken every one of his classes. In the year 2003, I graduated from Emerson with a Bachelor's degree in Theater Studies with an emphasis on both Acting and Costume Design. After I was told I was too young to begin my graduate degree, I began working in a shop sewing as well as doing some freelance design projects in Boston and working retail to make ends meet. Before I knew it, I was asked to move to New York and take a position in the buying office of French Connection. While at French Connection, I began taking draping classes at FIT. Today, I find myself not designing but working with designers as part of the buying team at Giorgio Armani. I owe much of my success to Rafael Jaen and his teachings."

■ MARK NEWMAN

Mark Newman is an award-winning journalist who was most recently the managing editor of *Entertainment Design* and *Lighting Dimensions* magazines. His career has spanned from television talk shows to an off-Broadway theatre's box office to numerous editorial jobs in New York City. A native of Alabama, he currently resides in Chillicothe, Ohio.

"Who am I anyway? Am I my resume?"—So goes the lyric from the opening number of "A Chorus Line" sung by an aspiring triple-threat. For aspiring theatre designers, the answer to the lyric is yes . . . and no. Design faculty at top colleges can easily see through the gloss of a slick portfolio. An attractive presentation is nice, but if the talent and the ability are not there the presentation is moot. (Excerpt from "Avoiding a Portfolio Imbroglio," by Mark Newman, *Entertainment Design*, October 1, 2004.)

■ KAREN PERLOW

Karen Perlow has been a freelance lighting designer since 1986. She is an instructor at the Massachusetts Institute of Technology, has been a Stage Source Board Member since 2002, received the 2003 IRNE Award for best lighting design, and was a Somerville Arts Council grant reviewer in 2002.

Figure 17.13
Karen Perlow's lighting design for "City of Angels," produced by the Boston Conservatory of Music in 2005.

Figure 17.14
Close-up of
Anthony Phelps'
portfolio page.

ANTHONY R. PHELPS

Anthony R. Phelps is the Associate Technical Director at Harvard University. He holds an M.F.A. in Design from Minnesota State University, Mankato. His teaching credits include the University of Kentucky and Bradley University. Design credits include Theatre L'Homme Dieu, The Publick Theatre, and The Old Log Theatre. His professional memberships include United Scenic Artists, the International Alliance of Theatrical Stage Employees (IATSE), and the United States Institute for Theatre Technology (USITT). Anthony is the founder and executive editor of *The Painter's Journal*.

BRIAN PRATHER

Brian Prather earned his M.F.A. at Brandeis University. His scenic work includes the premiere production of "Fuente" for the Barrington Stage Company, the premiere of "My Heart and My Flesh" for Coyote Theater at Boston Playwright's Theater, "Working" for Emerson Stage at the Cutler Majestic Theatre, "First Love" for StageWorks Hudson, and "Thief River" for the Barrington Stage Company.

CARRIE ROBBINS, COSTUME DESIGN

Carrie Robbins has designed more than 30 Broadway shows, including 2001's "A Class Act," "Grease" (Tony nomination, Best Costumes), "Over Here" (Tony nomination, Best Costumes), "Agnes of God," "Yentl," "Octette

Figure 17.15
Brian Prather's
scenic design
pencil rendering
for the musical
"Working"
produced by
Emerson Stage at
the Cutler
Majestic Theater
in Boston in 2005.

Figure 17.15
Brian Prather's scenic design pencil rendering for the musical "Working" produced by Emerson Stage at the Cutler Majestic Theater in Boston in 2005.

Bridgeclub," "Sweet Bird of Youth," "The First," "Frankenstein," "Happy End," "Boys of Winter," "Cyrano," "Shadow Box," "The Iceman Cometh," and "Secret Affairs of Mildred Wilde." Among her awards, she has won five Drama Desk Awards, a Maharam, and several international design awards. She has created designs for the Lincoln Center Repertory Theatre, Chelsea Theatre Center, Acting Co., and the New York Shakespeare Festival. Regionally, she has designed at Mark Taper Forum ("The Tempest," for which she received the F.I.T. Surface Design Award) and "Flea in Her Ear" (L.A. Dramalogue Award), Guthrie Theatre, and Williamstown. Her film and television work includes "In The Spirit," "SNL," PBS' "Arts in America" series, and several unseen pilots. Her opera designs include San Francisco Opera ("Samson et Dalila"), Houston Grand Opera, Sarah Caldwell's Opera Co. of Boston, Hamburg Statsoper, and Washington Opera. She was profiled in the text *Costume Design: Techniques of Modern Masters and Contemporary Designers*, among others. She has been a Master Teacher of Costume Design at New York University for more than 25 years. Her recent work includes *"Exact Center of the Universe"* for the Women's Project, *"Tallulah Hallelujah," "Toys in the Attic," "Rags"* (Paper Mill Playhouse), *"The Wedding Banquet," "Belle"* (directed by Tazewell Thompson), and currently *"White Christmas,"* a new musical based on the film, directed by Walter Bobbie and opening at the Curran Theatre in San Francisco in November 2006. She also designed uniforms for the restaurants The Rainbow Room and Windows on the World (which received the 1997 Image of the Year Award).

JULIANNE TAVARES

Julianne Tavares, a set designer and scenic charge/painter, earned her B.F.A. degree in Design–Technology in 2005 at Emerson College in Boston. She has worked on "Goodbye, Dolly" (Emerson), "Footloose" (RB Productions), and "Johnny Guitar" (BCA), in addition to painting for Opera Boston.

KRISTINA TOLLEFSON

Kristina Tollefson earned her M.F.A. in Costume Design and Technology from Purdue University, is currently an Assistant Professor and Resident Costume and Makeup Designer at the University of Central Florida in Orlando, and is also a member of United Scenic Artists Local 829. She serves as the Vice-Commissioner for Communication for the Costume Design & Technology Commission of the United States Institute for Theatre Technology.

Figure 17.16
From "Rags" (Papermill Playhouse, 1999), study for an immigrant woman drawn by Carrie Robbins using Painter and Photoshop.

Figure 17.17
Julianne Tavares'
portfolio page
layout that
includes set
model
photographs for a
produced show.

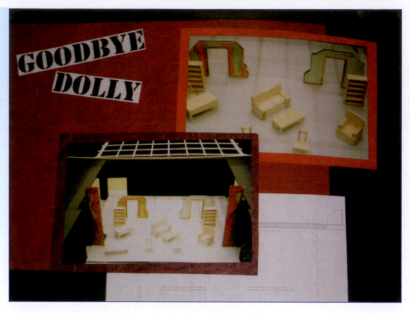

Figure 17.18
Kristina
Tollefson's digital
portfolio menu
page.

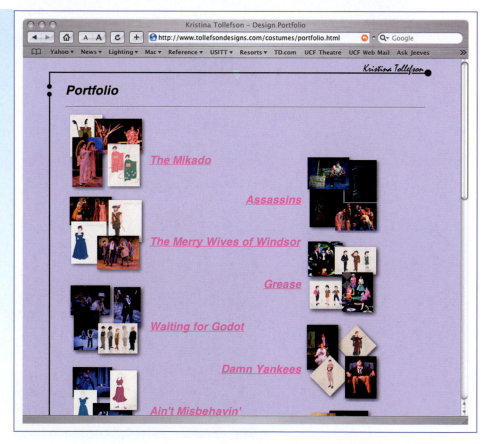

Figure 17.19
Nicholas Vargelis'
lighting design
photograph for
"The Idiot,"
produced at the
A.R.T. Institute for
Advanced
Theater Training
in 2004.

The Idiot adapted and directed by Alexandre Marine; Rogojin meets Nastasia Philipovna.
Scenic: Caleb Wertenbaker; Lighting: Nicholas Vargelis
A.R.T. Institute for Advanced Theater Training 6/2004

NICHOLAS D. VARGELIS

Nicholas D. Vargelis graduated *Magna Cum Laude* with a B.F.A. in Theater
Design Technology from Emerson College in 2003. At Emerson, he received
an EVVY Award for outstanding work in lighting design. He worked as a
freelance lighting designer in Boston and New York before going to Europe.
He is currently living in Berlin and has two upcoming photography exhibi-
tions: the first, a solo exhibit with a mix of work from the United States and
Paris; the second, a group showing focusing on his current work in Berlin.
Nicholas designed lighting in 2005 for an outdoor dance performance spon-
sored by the city of Berlin—a "night of arts" in NeuKolln.

Index